Being Right is not Enough!

How to take your improvement initiatives to the next level

By Gabriel Lopez Limon
with Fernando Lopez Sansalvador

authorHOUSE®

AuthorHouse™
1663 Liberty Drive
Bloomington, IN 47403
www.authorhouse.com
Phone: 1-800-839-8640

First published by AuthorHouse 1/20/2010

ISBN: 978-1-4490-4460-2 (e)
ISBN: 978-1-4490-4458-9 (sc)
ISBN: 978-1-4490-4459-6 (hc)

Library of Congress Control Number: 2009914333

Printed in the United States of America
Bloomington, Indiana

This book is printed on acid-free paper.

Dedication

To my parents, because I am;

to my grandfather, because of who I am;

to my wife and daughter, because of whom I am;

to God, for whom I am.

Gabriel

To my parents and brother, for their love, care and knowledge;

to my wife, for her love and support;

to my sons, for their being my life incentive;

to my friends, for the experiences we have shared;

to God, for the opportunity of a life experience.

Fernando

Contents

Foreword.

Occasionally, a consultant will write about his years of experience, distilling knowledge from his successes (and, yes, failures) into practical, how-to advice. This is often information that can't be gotten in any other way. Even if you could duplicate his experiences, you will never duplicate the years he has spent thinking and building intuition.

Very occasionally, such a book will also point us in a totally new direction for answers to urgent questions, not only providing us with valuable insights but – more important – provoking us to think. This book combines Fernando and Gabriel Lopez's years of experience, intuition, and success with a brilliant shift in thinking, all told in a personal and sincere style that speaks to their passion in helping people and companies to be successful. In short, it's everything I want in a business book.

But here's why I believe it will help you.

The number one competitive challenge facing companies today is change. As we work together in our companies, we must learn together how to adapt more and more quickly to new technologies and new ways of working, without losing those valuable elements that make us unique. We see many popular new systems and approaches, including Product Lifecycle Management, Theory of Constraints, Lean, Six Sigma, and many others. Promoters tell us how great their technology is. Sometimes they're right. But what they won't say is when the benefits will come, how long they will last, or how big the risks will be. They won't tell us where they may be wrong. So we understand without being told that other people are not always right, and that in order to successfully adopt their ideas we have to understand how these ideas may be right or wrong *for us*. When people tell us of the brilliance of their ideas and (therefore) how we should change, we never simply say, "Ok, I'll do it."

In this wonderful book, Fernando and Gabriel have verbalized this instinctive concept, that "being right is not enough," and applied it to the people who, sadly, are responsible for most of the problems we experience with change: ourselves. They hold up a mirror to show why it isn't enough for you or me to be right, even though we so often assume that it is (and we so often assume that we are). They show us how to be *more* right and *more* successful. If you study this book carefully, you will dramatically improve your ability to provoke change – in your company, your church, your family, anywhere you think other people should be paying more attention because *you're right*.

I could go on about the value of this book, the discussions of buy-in, sales, team building, urgency, and so on. But that would only keep you from getting started.

Read. Think. Continue to be right, but much more important, *be successful* – however you define success.

Rob Newbold

CEO, ProChain Solutions Inc.

Author of The Billion Dollar Solution and Project Management in the Fast Lane

Acknowledgments.

This book is about the untold stories of many people whose day-to-day efforts usually pass us by without any recognition or even awareness. Some of them are leaders of some kind of group; others are the brains and muscle that support those leaders in pursuing their dreams. It is them who give life to any improvement project, and it is their experiences and knowledge that we have attempted to synthesize in this book.

We have been blessed by coming in contact with so many of these fabulous individuals, who have made change a way of life, that it would be impossible to name them all. So, our first and biggest thanks go to all those who have shared with us their dreams and visions as change agents; their personal dramas as they attempt to make this a better world, and their tears and sorrows when things have not resulted as expected.

Our second blessing has come in the form of guides and tutors. People who have believed in us enough to share their knowledge and have the patience to explain it in as many different ways to make sure we got it. These are extraordinary people, because we are not precisely the easiest of audiences: Miguel Angel Bahena, Guido Cattaneo, Armando Enriquez, José Alfredo Esquivel, Fernando López Carmona, Carlo Martone, Oscar Morales.

The third blessing in our journey has been the magnificent group of companions who have been there to make sure that "no matter what" we all kept moving forward in the path to achieve our personal dreams: Ana María Alvarado, José Luis López, Rob Newbold, Bruno Acosta, Armando Delgado.

Finally, we would also like to take this opportunity to thank all the people at the Goldratt Institute and all other TOC practitioners who have had the courage to create a vision of their own, because by daring to face the complexities of independence, they have found and nourished the real value of collaborative work.

Introduction.

The Wise King

Once there ruled in the distant city of Wirani a king, who was both mighty and wise. And he was feared for his might and loved for his wisdom.

Now, in the heart of that city was a well, whose water was cool and crystalline, from which all the inhabitants drank, even the king and his courtiers; for there was no other well.

One night when all were asleep, a witch entered the city, and poured seven drops of strange liquid into the well, and said, "From this hour, he who drinks this water shall become mad."

Next morning all the inhabitants, save the king and his lord chamberlain, drank from the well and became mad, even as the witch had foretold.

And during that day the people in the narrow streets and in the market places did naught but whisper to one another, "The king is mad. Our king and his lord chamberlain have lost their reason. Surely, we cannot be ruled by a mad king. We must dethrone him."

That evening the king ordered a golden goblet to be filled from the well. And when it was brought to him, he drank deeply, and gave it to his lord chamberlain to drink.

And there was great rejoicing in that distant city of Wirani, because its king and its lord chamberlain had regained their reason.

- *Khalil Gibran*

Have you ever witnessed a heated discussion where you could not take sides because it seemed that all the participants were right? Or, have you ever been involved in an argument in which you were sure to be right, but could not get the others to follow your advice? Alternatively, as a leader (parent, boss, owner, etc.), have you been in the situation of knowing perfectly well what needs to be done, but could not get your people to do it right?

During our 20 years of experience as change agents in all sorts of organizations, we certainly have lived through a great number of scenes like the ones described above, and chances are that you have also gone through a fair deal of these kinds of situations in your own life.

What is the use of being right if nobody listens? Or, as in the short story at the beginning of this Introduction, what is the point of being wise and powerful if the rest of the world thinks we are mad?

Questions like these have been the recurrent topic of long conversations with Owners and Top Management of many kinds of organizations, as well as parents and Spiritual Leaders, all of whom have expressed great frustration about the impossibility to make their organizations and families perform according to what they consider to be "plain common sense".

The same complaint has been expressed constantly by members of the Academia and Young Professionals: What is the use of all the hours dedicated to study and researching the best solutions if at the end everyone ends up doing as they please?

Having listened very carefully to all the arguments presented by each of these persons, and having an external view of every particular situation, a common pattern began to emerge out of all the lamentations: All, absolutely all the persons manifesting their frustration on this matter were using as the base for their arguments the idea that: "being right should be enough for others to follow me and do as I tell them."

This discovery gave place to a series of studies, analysis and practical work that led us to the most significant finding of our experience promoting and guiding change in many different scenarios. We call it our "golden nugget legacy". This concept has allowed us to understand and guide improvement efforts through situations like the ones listed above and much worse.

As it always happens, once we have managed to decipher a complex problem, it turns out that the key to solving it seems to be such a simple thing, something that has been there all the time shouting out loud to be discovered. In no way our finding escapes this reality. In fact, we are absolutely sure that it is not even a discovery at all and that many people have come to this conclusion before ourselves.

Well, our golden nugget, the heart of this book and of our activities for the last ten years, is the realization, that although we have been educated, trained and conditioned to seek and defend being right, the reality is that although being right is important, BEING RIGHT IS NOT ENOUGH!

This realization is the result of our very own observations and discussions regarding improvement efforts in many different environments for which we have had first row seats: families, multinational organizations, self-owned businesses, sports teams, theater productions, universities, etc.

Observing the world through this new perspective, we find that the testimony is all around us in our everyday experiences.

How many times have you been totally sure of being right about something, determined to commit your time and money based on that assurance, and ended up confused and with no results -at least not the ones you wanted- to show for your efforts? The proof lies within the scars and tears of disappointment on all of us after banging our heads against the wall many, many times because we were sure to be right about something and thought we could act based on that knowledge only.

How many initiatives do you know of, that after spending much more time and money than originally planned, are still "in-process" or have been canceled? Proof is also in the millions of man-hours and dollars that are wasted every day in improvement projects that fail to deliver the expected results, even though they aimed at the "right" goals and were executed by the "right" people using the right procedures and spending the "right" amount of money.

How many people with a unique talent do you know that have had to give up their dream career in order to live in the "real world"? The proof, finally, is in the amount of dreams that are unachieved by the right people.

The proof is all around us and is overwhelming: BEING RIGHT IS NOT ENOUGH!

We feel confident that under this light, we can achieve consensus on the idea that we need to approach our improvement projects in a different manner. That something new has to be attempted if we want to be successful in promoting and guiding the necessary changes in our life and our organizations at the speed and with the effectiveness that our times are demanding. The amount of failures related to the total amount of changes initiated is too big to let it pass without questioning what is being done and looking for better ways to do it.

When we started our journey as change agents, we too assumed that finding the core problem, generating the right solution, and developing an achievable plan to reach it was all that was needed to move people and companies towards a better future. We assumed that being right was enough!

It was only after we lived through the experience of guiding change initiatives many times and seeing so many improvement efforts go through so much pain, that we had to ask ourselves: what is missing in our change model?, why do people drag their feet after we have shown them where the pot of gold is?

Of course, we started by blaming our clients. We used excuses like: "they are not giving us the right information", or "they are not committing enough resources, time or people to the project". But, in the privacy of our own offices, when we were all alone, we had to admit that there were cases when all of these arguments could not be applied at all. There were some clients who had given us their best people, their total commitment and dedication to the project, as well as access to all the information we had requested. And still, the process of change in these cases had been painful enough to make us doubt that the fault was on our clients.

Then we blamed our methodology. Surely, some step in the process was either badly executed by us, or was faulty by design. So, we went back to the books and classrooms. We assumed we needed more preparation. We have dedicated the last 15 years of our lives to study everything we have found related to changing efforts. We studied the business gurus' advice; Jack Welch, Peter Drucker, Michael Hammer, etc. We attended seminars on the latest improvement methodologies: Theory of Constraints, Six Sigma, Lean Manufacturing, Project Management, etc. We also searched in the self-improvement literature; we read Stephen Covey, Robert Kiyosaki, Benjamin Franklin, etc. We even considered texts related to metaphysics, neurolinguistics, mind mapping, creativity, etc. And once we were in the process of studying, we decided to re-visit the classics of philosophy and ethics: Socrates, Plato, Descartes, etc. In other words, our studies covered from business thinking to the human nature aspects of change.

All this knowledge improved tremendously the effectiveness of our interactions leading change efforts. However, the familiar sensation of difficulty while moving forward change projects was still there. People still said yes but acted like no.

If we had our client's best people and total commitment, and if we were using the most powerful methodologies and concepts related to guiding change, what was still missing?

Then, the realization dawned on us. We had been using a faulty assumption to create our change models all along. We had assumed that the real difficulty of change was in the proper analysis of the situation, in finding the core problem and its solution, and in developing the proper plan for its deployment. We had taken for granted the willingness and support of our people once we showed them that we had the right solution and a good plan to reach it. That was the reason why we had become experts on analyzing and deriving the best solutions our clients could have. We had turned ourselves into the Lords of the PowerPoint-Excel-Project universe and thus, we could demonstrate and convince even the most difficult audience that WE WERE RIGHT!

However, reality was shouting at us that this was not enough to make our projects move at the speed we had come to expect. Our model's basic assumption was incomplete. BEING RIGHT WAS NOT ENOUGH! Being right was only the beginning.

The deployment of the solution is as important as finding the solution, but experience was telling us that in most cases, tailoring and implementing the solution is a far more complex process than the diagnostic and planning steps. Thus, we had to start a new process of research and study.

First, we needed to understand why the assumption that being right is enough is so widespread. Why do so many people, of so many different backgrounds, assume that being right is enough? Why do so many of the improvement methodologies stop after the planning step? This understanding was very important to us, because if so many people share the same assumption, it must be because there is a very powerful reason to do so, and we cannot attempt to alter it, unless we know and deal with that reason.

Secondly, if being right is not enough, we had to find the key complements to the diagnostic and planning steps. If being right is not enough, then, what was missing in our change model to dramatically improve the performance and results of the change projects we were involved with?

At this point, we would like to place special emphasis on the word "enough". We will never attempt to claim that we have found the ultimate, full proof model to guiding change initiatives. In fact, for some people, telling them what needs to be done is enough for them to go and do it, and for some others, helping them to develop an achievable plan is enough to get them going.

Unfortunately, it is our experience that for most people and organizations, having a solution and the plan to achieve it is not enough. They need to go through some more steps after making a plan in order to start moving decidedly in the direction of the proposed change. How many more steps? We really do not know. We keep finding new elements that help us achieve better and faster results in our improvement projects. And we also know that it heavily depends on the nature of the proposed solution and the reality of the person or organization engaging in the desired change.

This book provides the elements that we have found to be enough to develop successful change models for most of the cases we have come across in our own experience. Enough to achieve better and faster results than the ones they have achieved so far. Enough to get them started in their own journey of self-improvement. But, definitely, there is still far too much that needs to be figured out with regard to managing change.

Through the first part of this book, we will share with you the elements that helped us come to the realization that BEING RIGHT IS NOT ENOUGH! Mostly, we will present them in the same chronological order in which we found them, because we believe that the sequence generated an evolutionary process that kept bringing forward to our consciousness the realization that one of our most basic assumptions as leaders and change agents was incomplete: BEING RIGHT IS NOT ENOUGH!

In the second part of the book, we provide an introduction to the most powerful concepts we have found to expand and complement our change model: Collaborative Work, Change Selling and the Continuous Review of Assumptions. Each of these chapters would in itself take a book (or many) to delve into all possible details of the topics covered. We present in this book only the most basic and practical elements to provide you with an initial guide into their understanding and use. Many references are provided for you to go into as much depth as you find necessary in your own journey.

As a final introductory note, we want to stress the point that if we claim that BEING RIGHT IS NOT ENOUGH!, not for a second do we attempt to convey the message that being right is of no importance whatsoever, and therefore, that you should not care whether you are right or not. We are not attempting to erase the need to be right, but rather to locate it in its correct place in our search for improvements.

Being right is a necessary quest, if nothing else, only because of the tremendous insight and understanding about life that is generated in the process of searching for the right answers. What we want to make you aware of is that being right is never the final point of anything, but the beginning of a fascinating and never-ending journey.

Chapter I. Bang your head as needed

"The left hemisphere is in charge of established knowledge and the right hemisphere is in charge of truly novel situations. That means that basically all of human life consists of cycles of learning characterized by encountering a new situation and then mastering it. So, that means that as you encounter a new situation, the right hemisphere kicks in first and then gradually there's a transition to the left hemisphere"
- Prof. Elkhonon Goldberg
New York University

Why is it so important for all us to be right? Why is the assumption that "being right is enough" so widely accepted? Why is it that most of us believes that having a good solution and a plan to reach it should be enough to get people excited and moving towards a better future?

Once we had come to the realization that BEING RIGHT IS NOT ENOUGH!, these questions haunted us for a long time. We had to go beyond that knowledge to be able to apply this new idea in reality.

We needed to find answers that could be used in practical, everyday activities. Having lived for a great deal of our lives fighting in the trenches of the operations' floor, we were conscious of the need for simple, powerful answers, that could be used in our day to day challenges as change agents.

Be aware that when we use the expression "day-to-day-challenges", we are by no means referring only to our professional work. As individuals, we also faced the education of our teenage kids, the complications that came with the aging of our parents, the effects in our marriage due to constant traveling, etc. Change was happening all around us, and we needed these answers to better deal with it.

We had a great advantage. Since there was so much change going on around us, we could put into practice almost immediately every concept that was presented to us. We did not do so in a totally scientific manner, but we tried every new concept separately, and we did observe and discuss in detail the resulting effects.

As we researched, studied, interviewed experts, and tested in practice every new idea, two things became very clear; first, we realized that the need to be right, and the assumption that being right is enough, are so strongly wired into our mind, not as a result of isolated, short lived happenings in our lives, but as a consequence of a life long process that starts when we are born, and gets reinforced everyday through our day to day, most basic, activities and experiences.

Secondly, we came to understand that if the need to be right, and the assumption that being right is enough, are so widely accepted, it had to be because both are the result of a very generic process that allows many people from different backgrounds to share the same beliefs regardless of their particular experiences and ways of life.

Thus, we concluded that there had to be a generic life process that could help us understand how the need to be right evolves in most of us to such a degree that it becomes one of our main drivers, and then how the assumption that being right is enough came to be so widely accepted.

Having reached this conclusion, the pieces of the puzzle started to fall into place, until we got a complete enough picture of what we have called: "The head-banging evolutionary process".

The name has its own story: When we started lecturing and coaching about change, one of our great motivators was the belief that we could save people from having to learn the same lessons in exactly the same manner we had come to learn them; by banging our head against problems time and again. We thought we would be doing people a favor by saving them from the pain of having to bang their heads as hard and as many times as we had.

Experience has shown us that we all need certain amount of head banging before we can grasp the real meaning of things. We realize now, that if we save one person from banging his head in one way, he or she will bang it in a different way. We have come to accept the fact that head banging is part of the natural process of learning about life.

Therefore, this account of the head banging evolutionary process has not as a primary objective to save you from banging your head in order to learn the lessons that are shared throughout this book. Its main purpose is to describe to you, in the most basic of ways, the life long process that generates and reaffirms our need to be right, as well as our belief that being right is enough.

Also, translating this process to implementing improvement initiatives can provide you with a way to identify the particular head banging processes that are involved in promoting and guiding change. We hope that by providing you with a map and a description of the different head banging stages involved in moving forward change initiatives, you can identify if your headaches are taking you in the right direction, or if you are simply banging your head randomly, looking very busy, but achieving very little.

1.1 The head banging evolutionary process.

As children, we have no conscience of right or wrong. We move, play and laugh for no other reason than because we feel like it. We do not stop to think about right or wrong, or about consequences, we simply act. In this frame of mind, we perform the most daring acts while living the richest learning period of our lives. It is in this stage of discovery that we develop our first concept of right and wrong: right, either produces pleasure or stops pain, while wrong generates pain or discomfort. We begin our process of learning right and wrong by banging our head against things.

Many specialists have told us that it is during the very first years of our lives that we develop our core values. Our parents, either consciously or unconsciously, become our strongest reference because our main goal at that age is to receive their love and approval.

This triggers a further refinement in our perception of right and wrong: "right", you get approved and loved; "wrong", you do not get approved or loved.

This is a very crucial moment in our lives. If we get too much attention and love, we might become spoiled, while too little approval and love can make us uncaring and resented for the rest of our lives. Finding the right balance is a very delicate matter and requires great attention from the parents.

Thus it is, that during childhood, we assume that being right is a prerogative of being an adult, and as a consequence, we look forward to becoming older. We observe and learn from our elders, we follow their example and attempt to copy their personalities because we want to be like them. We can hardly wait to be "grown ups". Boys use their father's shaving kits; girls try on their mother's shoes, and we all look forward to attending an adult conversation.

As we try to gain the love and approval from our elders, the concept of authority begins to appear more often in our lives. Now it is not only our parents telling us what to do and how to behave, but suddenly, there is also this immense array of people giving us orders and poking their noses into our lives all the time: Grand Parents, Older Brothers, Teachers, Coaches, Priests, Uncles, Police officers, Old Ladies, etc. We become more and more constrained and we can no longer move, play or laugh without somebody telling us that we are doing something wrong.

Getting loved or approved becomes more difficult and confusing every day, especially because all these people ask for different things, and they do not seem to give the same value to the same things. Getting an A in school can be totally right for our mother, while it can be non-interesting to our father. On the other hand, running into a fight can be a great thing to share with our father, while our mother would immediately scorns us for doing so.

Fortunately for us, youth endows us with an almost infinite amount of energy, which we tend to focus at gaining our freedom, challenging everything that has been imposed on us. Since by now we have some fifteen years of learning experience in life, we consider ourselves knowledgeable enough to play the game of right and wrong. After some years of following the instructions provided by those "who are right", we begin our process of independence by creating our own world, defining our own rules and openly challenging anyone who thinks differently. We assume that with passion and hard work, we can show the world how right we are. We also assume, that our righteousness will shield us from any harm that comes our way. Armed with this conviction, we start the fight for our independence banging our heads as hard and as frequently as we will not do in any other stage of our lives.

Then, a totally unexpected thing happens: The more we defend what we know to be right and the more we want to behave as our role models, the more opposition and lack of approval we get. All of the sudden, everyone and everything is totally against us. It is a very confusing time in our lives. People are telling us what to do all the time, but they always behave in a different manner.

When we dare to ask for explanations, either we are sent to the other side of the galaxy accompanied by our mother, or we are given a long and convoluted speech that usually includes a short segment about how somebody (you know, a friend of a friend ...) messed up his life doing what we want to do, and then a very long segment full of quotations, about how we should become the living image of virtue because they do not want us to make the same mistakes they or somebody else (the friend of a friend) has done.

Communication becomes totally distorted, what they say is utterly incomprehensible to us, and they always interpret what we say in the worst possible manner. We cannot stand the sight of them, and they feel exactly the same about us, except that they cannot help their need to meddle in our lives. We bang everybody's heads, and everybody bangs ours. It is an all-open head banging war.

All this head banging takes us to the realization that being right is not as simple as we thought. We discover that being right has far more shades than just white or black. We also discover that even though people are always giving advice about the need to do the right thing, they find it very difficult to apply that very same advice to themselves. Benjamin Franklin provides us with a terrific insight into this matter in his book "The Art of Virtue" (*1):

> "As the happiness or real good of men consists in right action, and right action cannot be produced without right opinion, it behooves us, above all things in this world, to take care that our own opinions of things be according to the nature of things. The foundation of all virtue and happiness is thinking rightly"

> "It was about this time (1728) that I conceived the bold and arduous project of arriving at moral perfection. I wished to live without committing any fault at any time; I would conquer all that either natural inclination, custom, or company might lead me into. As I knew, or thought I knew, what was right or wrong, I did not see why I might not always do the one and avoid the other. But I soon found I had undertaken a task of more difficulty than I had imagined. While my care was employed in guarding against one fault, I was often surprised by another; habit took the advantage of inattention; inclination was sometimes too strong for reason. I concluded, at length, that the mere speculative conviction that it was in our best interest to be completely virtuous, was not sufficient to prevent our slipping; and that the contrary habits must be broken, and good ones acquired and established, before we can have any dependence on a steady, uniform rectitude of conduct"

Being right then, is most definitely not as straightforward as becoming older. And what is worse is that in due time, we also discover that being right is a matter of perception. It seems that although we want to believe in universal truths, in day to day life, when we are not discussing life or death issues, but rather simple things like what movie we should watch this evening, we are faced with the realization that other people have different ideas that totally challenge our perception of what is right. Some more head banging is needed in order to learn that the laws of relativity also apply to being right.

Having reached adulthood, and finding that this does not at all imply that we are always right, (as we thought when we were young), we come to the conclusion that being right is not a matter of age, but a matter of power. We discover the self-feeding cycle: being right gives people power, and power allows people to be and do what they consider to be right. Since we humans are fascinated by power, we obviously develop a strong desire to be powerful in order to be always right.

Thus, being right becomes about winning, about showing others that we are right and they are wrong. Some people even care more about winning than about actually being right, because, why bother being right if all you need is to show others that they are wrong?

Following this rationale we start a new process in search of power. We must beat everything and everyone to gain the holly grail of righteousness: POWER. No amount of head banging will deter us from reaching this goal.

All of us will eventually make it to some kind of position with power. We will become mothers, supervisors, leaders, etc. Without us really noticing, a miraculous transformation will take place. Little by little, the power inherent to our positions will take over our minds until one day, perhaps even to our own surprise, we begin to use the most powerful argument of all times: "because I am your mother (or boss, or whatever)!" Which means, that all attempts to rationalize with us are a waste of time, and that our next argument in line will be the brute use of our power in whatever form we might have at hand, the ammunition varying from worn out shoes to nuclear weapons of mass destruction.

We all know the story of the emperor that ended up naked in front of all his subjects because nobody dared telling him that his new clothes were non-existent. This happens with such regularity in everyday life, that one has to wonder whether we really get the message of the tale. As visitors in many organizations, we have watched many times as leaders run "naked" around their organizations, giving orders here and there, always getting affirmative responses from their people, just to see how, as soon as the boss gets back into her or his office, everyone goes back to what they think is more important.

We can confidentially tell you that, at our own times, we were also seduced by the sweet delusion of rightfulness provided by hierarchical power. Who dares telling the boss that he or she is utterly wrong? How many times are you willing to defend an argument against the opinion of the person in charge of your promotions and quality of work? After some time of nobody challenging our arguments, and many people telling us how clever we are, we actually begin to believe that we might, after all, be right all of the time. Once we get used to this status of infallibility, we begin acting as if everything we think and say is really unique and clever. We totally forget that there is no better mix for failure than arrogance and an "I-know-everything" attitude. How is it that most leaders get to discover that they are not infallible? By banging their heads against unforeseen problems in almost every aspect of their lives.

1.2 The unhappy ending

It is through this life long evolutionary process that we get so enthralled into the "being right" game. We place the "I am right" argument in such a high pedestal that being right in itself becomes our ultimate goal.

As most experienced leaders will tell you, reaching positions of power is by no means the final solution. There is plenty of head banging still to come as we develop our abilities to promote and guide change efforts.

For some people, this represents the search for more power. They assume that more and more power will eventually allow them to be right all of the time. Or maybe, the solution is another kind of power; instead of hierarchical power, some people are looking for "beauty" power. Or perhaps, media power, army power, religious power or whatever other form of power you might think of. It really does not matter, the point is to get it and make use of it.

We can easily understand why the world is in the state that it is now if every single person is searching for more and more power, and is willing to pay whatever price is required.

To make matters even more interesting, being right becomes so elusive, that we must spend far too many hours thinking, discussing, trying and fixing our approaches to being right. The end result is that, at the end of the day, we just do not have the time or energy to realize that, if anything, being right is only the first step that leads to a long journey, that just BEING RIGHT IS NOT ENOUGH!

Why do we claim that it is not enough? Because we keep banging our heads against all sorts of problems. Because despite all we know about being right, we have not been able to avoid pain and discomfort at will, yet.

But above all, we know it is not enough because we hear more and more about people performing the most horrendous acts simply because they do not feel loved or accepted. And that (being loved and accepted) was precisely what gave birth in all of us to the concepts of right and wrong.

Chapter II. Change requires a sense of urgency

"The truly creative mind in any field is no more than this: A human creature born abnormally, inhumanely sensitive. To them... a touch is a blow, a sound is a noise, a misfortune is a tragedy, a joy is an ecstasy, a friend is a lover, a lover is a god, and failure is death.

Add to this cruelly delicate organism the overpowering necessity to create, create, create -- so that without the creating of music or poetry or books or buildings or something of meaning, their very breath is cut off...

They must create, must pour out creation. By some strange, unknown, inward urgency, they are not really alive unless they are creating"
- Pearl Buck

In the last chapter we described how our constant search for love and acceptance gives birth and reaffirms, throughout all of our lives, the need to be right. This need evolves, from a very simple concept -right produces pleasure, wrong generates pain-, to a far more complicated set of rules and beliefs used in a constant search for power.

We also showed that rather than an evil-minded lust for power, this is a natural process that, given the normal complexities of life, happens to most of us while we attempt to generate our well being.

We now know why and how the need to be right takes such precedence in our lives, as well as why it is so widely accepted. We could, as a consequence, begin to talk about searching for possible solutions. In fact, that is usually the agreed upon way; once a problem is defined and its causes identified, we ought to develop a reasonable plan to transform our current reality into the desired future.

But remember, BEING RIGHT IS NOT ENOUGH! Knowing what is the problem is not enough. Before we spend any time looking for answers and falling in love with them, we must produce a key element to bring change about at the desired speed. We must create a sense of urgency to solve the problem.

No, do not fool yourself assuming that having identified the problem and understood its causes will be enough to inspire people to take action. Experience has shown us that without a sense of urgency, change either does not happen at all or it happens at far too slow a rate as to be of any real good.

We first encountered the need to consider the urgency of matters in Stephen Covey's marvelous book "The Seven Habits of Highly Successful People" (*2) We have all fallen victims to the trap of centering all our attention in the urgent matters and paying no attention to the important, usually non-urgent, matters.

It is the classic dilemma between solving the short term versus solving the long term. Yes, we know we should take action on both. But knowing it is not enough, because today's problems are hurting us here and now. We feel that, unless we take immediate action to solve the most urgent matters, there will be no future at all to think about.

So, we try to get rid of the most urgent problems to be able to attend the long term ones appropriately. Unfortunately, as we fight to keep abreast of today's problems, we find a never ending supply of urgent problems that leaves no time or energy to deal with the important, long term, matters.

The solution was provided to us by Robert C. Newbold (*3), an expert in project management: We must make important matters urgent. We must develop a "burning platform" environment in which people either jump, fly or die.

Without a burning platform scenario, most people will try to stick to the old ways, simply because that is what they know well. Even if they complain about them all the time! Keeping in existence a known environment provides us with a sense of security, because however bad it might be, we already know what to expect and how to react. Besides, there is always the possibility that a different one might be worse.

In practice, we have identified a number of different approaches to create a burning platform scenario. Some leaders generate it by identifying or creating crisis situations. Others do it by setting very aggressive goals and punishing people hard for not meeting them. We are sure you can add some examples of your own.

However, there are two important things to bear in mind. First, you must be aware that creating crisis situations just for the sake of it is a great recipe to bring about total chaos in your organization. You do not want to generate a situation in which all of your people are running around crashing with one another, breaking every rule or moral principle to save their jobs.

The burning platform scenario we are talking about implies a sense of urgency, but towards a clear common enemy. A sense of urgency not only to act, but rather to act as a well coordinated team. The leader cannot just generate the crisis scenario and leave. She or he must remain deeply involved in coordinating all decision making and the resulting execution.

The second key aspect of the burning platform scenario is that it cannot be used as a regular resource for everyday activities. Too much of a good thing does not lead to a better thing. For everyday activities, you must have in place efficient procedures that make sure work is done fast and well on a regular basis.

Making use of the burning platform scenario for these kinds of activities will get your people used to the sense of urgency, which will then become the regular environment and, since not everything can be urgent all the time, we go back to not having a real sense of urgency at all. Everything then will be labeled as urgent and you will have to start classifying matters as extra-urgent and super-urgent, which means this resource has been burned out.

In our work as change agents, although the approach changes to suit the personality of the organization, we tend to generate this sense of urgency through the development of clear connections between the problem identified and its consequences in the short, medium and long term.

Please take note that it ought to be done not only for the long term consequences, and not only for the short-term implications, it must be done for both! Ideally, we would love to know that whatever action we take now, will have a positive impact in current emergencies, as well as helping to develop the future we desire.

In order to create a sense of urgency to adopt the proposed new paradigm that BEING RIGHT IS NOT ENOUGH!, we will examine the most likely consequences of keeping the assumption that being right is enough as the base for our decisions and actions.

If being right is still our driving force, four basic scenarios come to mind with regard to our responsibilities as change agents:

2.1 You are right, they are wrong

We chose to discuss this scenario first because it is by far the most common of the four. Most of us tend to believe that we are right, and that it is usually "the others" who are wrong. Who are the others? Anyone who has an opinion different from ours.

For discussion's sake, let us assume that it is possible to be right on everything all of the time. That would be great, would it not? Ideally, if we could be right all the time, we would not have to worry about any of our decisions because we would know that whatever we decide it would be right. People would know that we never fail and would ask for our advice on important matters.

Well, we have seen it happen, if only for given periods of time; Presidents, General Managers, Parents, Geniuses, Rock Stars, etc., all get to live the case of temporary infallibility. We get to be right all the time while our power to back up our decisions lasts.

Under the infallibility cloak, we have total clarity of what should be done or said in every situation. There is not one single matter in which we do not have an opinion about how it could be done better. We get to believe that we know even more than the experts on their very subjects.

Unfortunately, the number of things we can do on our own are very limited. For most things, we will need to interact with other people to get things done. Living in an ever more complex society, we have to play many different roles for which we have different degrees of control.

When we are always right and the rest of the world is always wrong even the simplest of things becomes a very frustrating experience. We ask for things and they do not happen. We explain and people do not get it. We demand and people consider us a monster. In the end, we prefer to isolate ourselves in order to avoid further frictions and frustration.

Sooner or later, we discover than being always right, instead of bringing the respect and trust of other people, seems to generate exactly the opposite reaction. Eventually, people start avoiding us. People may even admit later that what we said was perfectly right, but they would still rather go around us to make their own decisions.

What is the price to be paid for being always right? Utter loneliness. Who wants to be, talk or live with someone who is always right? It might be because we always disagree on what other people think. Or maybe it is because they hate to find out that what we say is always right. It could even be because they feel embarrassed for not following our advice. The fact is, that as time goes by, even our family deserts us.

In the past, people who were considered to have the gift of infallibility (like the oracle for the ancient Greeks), even had to live outside of the city, because they were "odd" with regard to the rest of the population.

In today's world, the form of isolation has become far more sophisticated. These kinds of people have created their own private clubs or societies away from the rest of the world, in which they reaffirm the importance of being right all the time, and they comfort each other in their solitude.

Sure, we will always have the consolation of knowing that we are right. But, what good is that if we cannot get things to happen?, or if we end up all alone? Being always right, while the others are always wrong, instead of helping us achieve many things, becomes a huge barrier to our success.

BEING RIGHT ALL THE TIME, WHEN THE OTHERS ARE ALWAYS WRONG, IS NOT ENOUGH!

2.2 You are wrong, they are right

Considering the point of view of a normal person, the one who is not right all the time, we can imagine that the opposite scenario comes to life. There is always little clarity as to what should be done or said in any situation. Doubt is present at every step. Some pushy people come to tell us what must be done, but we are not sure. We always want more time to think about it. Then she or he explains his reasons, and they sound perfectly sound, but still, we want to make sure they apply to us. Then he or she looses his or her temper and demands that we take action, which either forces us to enter a fight with that person, or to do something of which we are not totally convinced of, almost ensuring its doom from the start.

The last thing we need is one of those "know-it-alls" telling us what it is we should be doing. It is not as if we love to be wrong. We are already banging our head heavily against life because nothing seems to go our way, our career is going down the drain, and we might even feel uglier and more repulsive than the Hunchback of Notredame. Clearly we would welcome the chance to be right at least once.

If every promising step ends up leading to disappointment and more trouble, why should it matter to us whether being right is enough or not? Well, we strongly believe that you have already discovered that BEING

RIGHT IS NOT ENOUGH!, but have not yet been able to find a way out of your current situation using that knowledge.

As change agents, we have come to accept as a fundamental truth that, in her or his everyday life, every person is always trying her or his best to be right. We have not yet found a person who comes to us accepting that his goal in life is to be wrong. Just as it is practically impossible to be always right about everything, it is as unlikely that one person can be wrong all the time.

We have seen so many right initiatives generate negative outcomes; we have counseled so many leaders with the right ideas and attitude who could not get beyond six months in their jobs. And, by the same token, we have watched many times incredulously as apparently wrong solutions turned out to produce wonderful results. We can assure you: It is not because we are not right that things are not going our way, it is mostly because being right is not enough that things are not working as we expected.

No, of course we cannot claim that we are never wrong, that would be unrealistic. Or that we should aim to be wrong to produce great results. That would be irresponsible and suicidal. What we are saying is that, if things are not going our way, it is for the most part, the result of the fact that being right is not enough rather than because we have been wrong all the time.

When our boss wins every argument, is not necessarily because she or he is right and we are not; it is more likely that his point of view prevails only because she or he has the power to enforce it. When a bully gets his way and we do not, it is not because he is right and we are not; it is because we prefer to avoid a physical confrontation.

Therefore, it is not then a matter of who is right and who is not. It is a question of who has the most power to enforce her or his point of view. We might not have the upper hand now, but we know that sooner or later the tables will turn, and then we will make sure that those who imposed their beliefs on us will pay the price.

Being always wrong, while the others are always right, is the perfect ground to grow frustration and resentment, which will drive us to become as huge an obstacle as we possibly can to anyone else's' initiatives for improvement. Why should we let them be successful when we are not?

BEING WRONG ALL THE TIME, WHEN THE OTHERS ARE ALWAYS RIGHT, NOT ONLY IS NOT ENOUGH, IT IS DISASTROUS!

2.3 You are wrong, they are wrong

The most usual consolation for everyone is to think that, in the end, nobody is right. It is logical to conclude that if we cannot be right all the time, then nobody else can; therefore, it is safer to assume that we must all be wrong to begin with.

That is, we all take as a starting position in any discussion, the "show me" attitude. We all have our own point of view; we know the other person will most likely not go along with it, so we let him show his cards first. Then, all we have to do is to invalidate his arguments and present ours as the ones to be taken, not because they are right, but because at that point, that will be the only alternative left.

The problem is that we have all played this game many times before. We know what is coming. We have already developed a number of tactics to evade providing our arguments first, so we show only a part of them, or start by explaining a misleading argument, or we present some ideas based on what we think the arguments of the other person are, or any other tactic that will allow us to safeguard our arguments while we attempt to prove everybody else's are wrong.

You can easily imagine what effects this kind of maneuvering has in achieving proper communication. We could fill hundreds of pages describing the most incredible discussions we have witnessed as change agents: Husband and wife claiming that each has lived twenty years of marriage doing what the other wants, and never getting their own way;

Partners complaining that they do much more for their business than any other partner; Managers handling their areas as small kingdoms ready to attack any of his fellow managers who dares trespassing on his dominions.

Surely, this kind of environment is not precisely the proper one to make an organization lean and efficient. In the end, regardless of how grand the situation was at one time, the organization (marriage, business, soccer team, etc.) falls apart. Which brings about the final proof of the starting assumption: we were all wrong.

And since we are all wrong, cynicism begins to develop in our minds. What is the point of doing anything if it will not work anyway? Why should we do what management says if in the end they will change their mind? Why should we follow instructions if nothing happens to those who don't? When any initiative for positive change is met with complete cynicism under the banner of "this company will never change", then the countdown for extinction has already begun.

The odd thing is, that just as being right is not enough to guarantee the success of an enterprise, it is also true that being wrong is not enough to bring down an organization. It takes far more than one mistake, even if it is humongous, to destroy a company. It is only when the day-to-day operations become plagued with distrust and resentment that the real downfall begins.

Mistakes can hurt the performance of any organization, but they are seldom enough on their own to cause its end. On the other hand, when everyone in the organization is trying her or his best to ensure that everyone else is wrong, this will indeed ensure a premature demise of even the healthiest of companies.

EVERYONE BEING WRONG IS MORE THAN ENOUGH TO KILL ANY INITIATIVE.

2.4 You are right, they are right

Out of the four possible scenarios, this is by far the least used by most people, mainly because at some point in our lives, we have come to believe that there is only one possible right answer for every question. Thus, whenever someone presents a point of view that is different from ours, an automatic defense mechanism is activated: "One of the two must be wrong". And since we know our opinion to be right, it is usually the "other's" ideas that seem wrong to us.

The possibility of both of us being right does not cross our minds at all. However, the key to reach beyond the assumption that being right is enough, is precisely the understanding that it is perfectly possible for two or more points of view to be both right and opposed, at the same time.

Is it possible for you and your boss to be both right, even though your suggestions are against each other? The answer is YES! Is it possible for you and your teenage daughter to be both right despite the abysmal differences in your positions? Again, the answer is YES! Is it possible that our political parties are all right, despite the completely opposing proposals on every single issue? ... well, not really, that would be stretching our argument too much.

The realization that two opposing arguments can be equally right is so important, that we have dedicated a whole chapter to it (What does being right mean?). A whole universe of new possibilities appears before our eyes just by removing the assumption that "there is only one right answer for every situation".

When there are many right answers, then it really does not matter who is right. Instead of using our time and energy in destroying each other's points of view, we can concentrate in adding our perspectives and taking action. And even if we discover that we were wrong, we can correct our solution faster and with far less effort and resources.

No other change of paradigm can be as powerful to unlock the vastness of this life. True riches lie for those who can endeavor in this world using this paradigm as the basis for managing their relationships with others. Why? Well, because at every turn in life, they will always have lots of people willing to work with them.

2.5 Do you want to change something? Let's run!

We have shown you the four different scenarios of consequences if we continue using the idea that being right is enough as the basis for our decisions and actions. As you have seen, three out of the four end up in frustration and loneliness, while only the fourth one shows a positive outcome. Which one of them would you rather have defining your future?

The good news is that you do not have to wait many years to see the results of this approach. We can tell you that almost immediately you will begin to experience life in a totally new way.

The bad news is that it will not be easy. Changing a rooted paradigm is one of the most difficult things to accomplish in this life. Not because of lack of desire or inner strength, but, simply because it implies changing our whole position in this world and that, besides being utterly difficult, it is very scary.

Being totally honest and based on our experiences guiding this kind of paradigm change, we could predict that if we start acting now, it will take anything between five to ten years to produce and become comfortable with the new paradigm and its corresponding patterns of behavior.

No, we do not know of any pill or seminar that can generate such change overnight. We would love to be able to offer a miracle device or program to induce this kind of change faster, since we are convinced this world needs it fast.

God knows we have attempted many times to take what seemed like plausible shortcuts in the pursuit of reducing these times. After many failed attempts, we have come to the realization that this kind of change demands a certain period of gestation in order to allow us to understand and assimilate all the adjustments that are implied. Asking three women to bear a child does not mean that we can have a baby in three months.

We are fully aware that this may be a piece of devastating news for many people. What do you mean it takes years to adopt and become comfortable with this new paradigm? Mind you, this statement does not imply in any way that we will not see any results until then. We have already expressed that most likely, you will begin to see positive outcomes as soon as you start working towards reaching this objective.

Our aim is to avoid complacency with the initial results. If we stop persevering, the necessary changes to truly create a clear competitive advantage will not be completed. Remember that the great masterpieces that inspire us and have transcended over time, were not made in one day, but were the result of great patience and dedication from their authors.

The only secure recipe we know so far is hard and clever work during a long enough period of time. Therefore, if you really want to create a positive future for you and your organization (family, business, or whatever), we must start acting right now to produce the necessary changes to make it happen.

Let us begin unraveling what is needed to live under the paradigm that BEING RIGHT IS NOT ENOUGH!. Let's run together!

Chapter III. What does "being right" mean?

> **Morpheus:** *Do you want to know what IT is? The Matrix is every-where. It is all around us, even now in this very room. You can see it when you look out your window or when you turn on your television. You can feel it when you go to work, when you go to church, when you pay your taxes. It is the world that has been pulled over your eyes to blind you from the truth.*
>
> **Neo:** *What truth?*
>
> **Morpheus:** *That you are a slave, Neo. Like everyone else you were born into bondage, born into a prison that you cannot smell or taste or touch. A prison for your mind.... Unfortunately, no one can be told what the Matrix is. You have to see it for yourself. This is your last chance. After this there is no turning back. You take the blue pill, the story ends, you wake up in your bed and believe whatever you want to believe. You take the red pill, you stay in Wonderland, and I show you how deep the rabbit hole goes.... Remember, all I'm offering is the truth, nothing more.... Follow me...*
>
> **- The Matrix**

According to the dictionary, being right means: "complying with justice, correctness or reason; correct, just, true." Since justice, correctness and reason, are fundamental principles, on which a great number of attitudes and behaviors towards life are based, we tend to assume that what is just, correct and true has a universal value. For instance, we believe that delivering on time, providing good services, offering competitive prices, etc., are equally valid anywhere in the world. Therefore, we tend to assume that there has to be a set of principles that must rule the behavior of persons and organizations who wish to be successful, and thus, that there has to be one, and only one way to be right. One way that must be superior and better than all others.

Whenever we bring up this subject in all kinds of audiences, but mainly when we do it before leaders and owners of organizations, there is usually a murmur of consent towards the idea that people either is right or not. How else would it be possible to take decisions? In which other ways could they judge about an investment of capital or about a reduction on their resources? Being right is considered one of those black or white subjects in which there cannot be anything in the middle. When it comes to these matters, there seems to be no possible scale of grays.

Sure, being right is one of those binary issues with only two possible values, yes or no. But it is only so when we talk about them. More to the point, they are only black or white when we talk about them applying them to someone else.

Whenever we dig a little deeper in the way someone is actually using in his own life a concept for which she or he has already agreed that there are no possible deviations from what is considered to be right, like not telling lies, we find that most of us, have already accepted ways to make exceptions to the rule for our particular case. It is not as if we are professional liars. It is only that we are very good at finding attenuating circumstances when it comes to us. But when it comes to passing judgment on others, we return to the scenario in which yes or no are the only possible answers.

3.1 The laws of relativity apply to what is right

It is clear that when we enter into life and death matters, very clear dividing lines appear in our minds, and the same goes for a given number of issues. But, we have observed that there are a far greater number of topics for which definite boundaries between right and wrong are not so clear. Particularly, this is true for hundreds of tasks that must be performed on a day-to-day basis by most of us.

For instance; should we give the client a discount or not?; should we fire an employee for breaking the rules to satisfy a client's request?; should we lend our car to our seventeen year old son?

The answer for all of the above questions is: "it depends" It depends on the specific situation that each question is referring to. We need more information in order to be able to form our judgment.

But still, when more information is provided, different people will provide different answers. The reason is that to form our decision, there is usually more than one value or belief that must be taken into account. We must develop a decision mixing different concepts, feelings and values, for which, each of us has a different perception, resulting from on our own experiences in life.

Offering discounts to clients is not really a decision that will be based on whether discounts are right or wrong. The decision will be formed using our past experiences not only about discounts, but also about our particular history with this client, the current situation of the market, the information we have about our competitor's activities, and so on. The final decision will be based on a very complex mixture of perceptions regarding each one of the aspects that we have considered relevant for making this specific decision.

You can easily imagine that different people will consider relevant different aspects for their decision-making. Then, depending on our own situation, we will all have different perceptions about each one of those aspects. And finally, we will for sure generate a different mixture of values-perceptions-logic which will result in a different answer to the same question.

When we get lucky, the answers are similar, which can generate an easy agreement on the final decision. However, most of the times, the answers tend to be different, even oppose each other, and then the shoot-out begins.

It is easy to understand then why it is so straight forward for the finance people to deny any discount to a client they have never met, while it is always the first suggestion coming from the sales people, who have developed a close relationship with the client, and for whom the sale represents an important part of their income.

3.2 The three dimensional reality

One of our favorite exercises when working with groups consists of presenting them with a sealed box containing a figure. The box is a perfect cube and the only way to look into its content is through two little holes placed on two different sides. From one hole, the participants will see a rectangle. From the other one, they will see a circle.

We ask all of the participants but one to use one specific hole to look into the box and then write what they saw -let us say the rectangle-. Then we ask the remaining attendee to look through the other hole and write down his observation -the circle for our example-.

When we ask them what they saw, the response is unanimous. A rectangle! Many times, the person who saw the circle will not even dare to say that he saw something different until we push him to do so. When he produces a different result than the rest of the group, usually there is a brief moment of silence, but then he gets battered by his peers about his lack of knowledge on geometry. How can he be such a fool not to identify a rectangle?

After some moments, we ask them to come to a unanimous decision about the content of the box. Then, the funniest thing happens; nine times out of ten, someone will propose voting as the mechanism to come to a unanimous decision! What a surprise!

In ten years of running this exercise, not one single group has come to the conclusion that what it is inside of the box is not a rectangle or a circle, but a cylinder. Not one single time have they thought about adding their results to form a more complete answer. They assume immediately that, because they are different, one of them has to be wrong.

The objective of this game is to make the participants aware that according to basic geometry, every single point in space can be seen from at least three different angles -x,y,z-, that this may produce dramatically different views, but also that all of them might be right at the same time. It is only when we add all three results that we can develop a more complete picture of reality.

In everyday decisions, there are far more possible points of view than just three. Discounts to clients can surely be seen one way from the sales department's point of view, in a very different way by the production people, in another one by the finance group and yet in quite a different manner from corporate headquarters.

Unless we come together and share our pieces of knowledge, we will never have a complete picture of reality, and as a consequence all our decisions will be based on incomplete data or, more often than not, by pure gut feeling.

3.3 The reality model

Being right then is a matter of what point of view we have. It is a matter of perspective, and our perspective is determined by everything that happens to us during our lifetime.

In his book, "Gaining control", Robert F. Bennett (*4) presents a wonderful tool to help us become aware of the needs and principles driving our patterns of behavior. He calls it, "The Control Model". In it, he explains how our results are the consequence of our patterns of behavior, that are generated by the rules we have set, which are determined by our principles' system, that is in its turn triggered by our needs. (See Fig 1.)

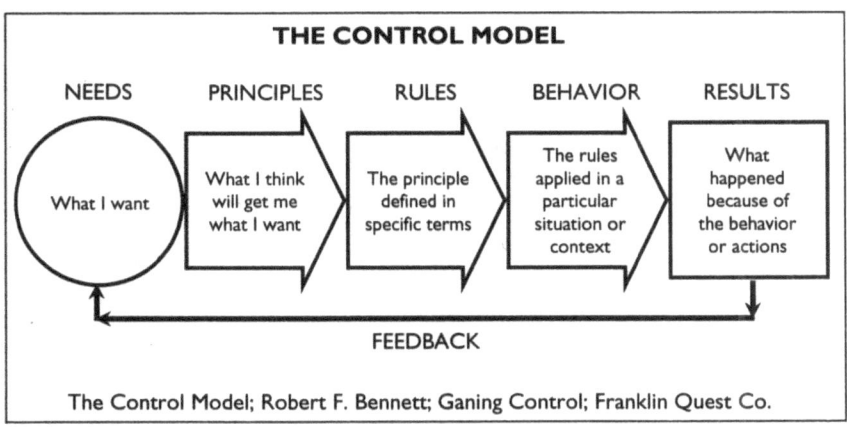

Fig 1.

He describes that, based on our most unsatisfied need, a chain reaction is started, ending up in certain results that may or may not satisfy our original need. If the result is a certain degree of satisfaction on such need; the principles, rules and behaviors used are confirmed as valid, and therefore, get reaffirmed in our mind. If the opposite is true, if the result was that our triggering need remained unsatisfied or got worse; then we start questioning the validity of the principles, rules and behaviors used.

Although the whole model is very powerful, there are two specific elements to which we would like to draw your attention; the wheel representing our needs and the belief window depicting our principles' system.

According to the model, we try to keep satisfied all our basic needs. However, most of the time, there is a lack of balance between them, resulting in one of them being the most unsatisfied of all. This need then takes a commanding place in our minds and our belief window sorts all our core principles according to their impact on the satisfaction of that specific need. For example, if our need to be loved is the most unsatisfied of all our basic needs, then our belief window will give priority to all our principles and values related to being loved.

Once a specific need has taken the commanding place in our minds and our brain has sorted out our principles and beliefs according to the satisfaction of that need, the rest of the model is activated to drive our actions towards the fulfillment of the targeted need. We become hypersensitive to everything related with the satisfaction of this need and we pay particular attention to all possible means of satisfying it.

The significance of this cause and effect relationship is paramount to our discussion, because it clearly shows that what is right, even for the same person, varies, according to the specific need that she or he is trying to satisfy at any given point in time.

If we are attempting to satisfy our need to love and be loved, skipping a day of work might seem like the right decision, while, if our need for professional self esteem is the one in the driving position, the thought of missing one day at work might never cross our minds.

3.4 The need to agree on agreeing

What is right then, depends on both, the internal and the external circumstances that must be taken into account at the specific moment of making any given decision. And since circumstances are subject to interpretation, each person is likely to generate a very unique conclusion for the same situation, given their unique experiences in life, as well as the specific amount and type of information they have at the moment of making their decision. It is of little surprise then, that given a problem, people in an organization will promote different approaches and different solutions.

However, the real problem does not stem from the fact that there will always be many different solutions put forward for the same problem. What really complicates, and very often destroys any possibility to develop a valid solution, is the assumption that there has to be ONE right solution for each problem.

Believing that there has to be ONE right solution for each problem brings in all the negative behavioral patterns we have described in the previous chapters. Instead of adding to our points of view, everyone will attempt to destroy everybody else's ideas in an all-against-all fight to show who is really right.

The saddest thing about this mechanism is that everyone will be so good at destroying each other's suggestions that, in the end, none of the ideas presented would seem worth being tried, leaving the organization paralyzed on that subject.

Therefore, the first step in promoting and guiding change is agreeing to agree. We must surrender the need to be right to the higher objective of making our organizations truly successful or even just to save them. In the end, as leaders, that is what we are really responsible for: to take care of the interests of our shareholders, our clients, our employees and our society, before our own.

As Keith R. McFarland explains in his book "The Breakthrough Company" (*5):

> "Leader's must be willing to "crown the company". In other words, they must put the interests of the firm above their own, harnessing the power of people at all levels in building the firm's future"

Harnessing the power of people means that we must develop the ability to generate the sum of talents, for which it is essential to understand that there is always more than one possible valid solution for every single problem.

Which one is chosen will vary for every specific set of circumstances. What is important is not which proposal is taken, but rather, to make sure that every member of the team will back it up as if it was his or her own. We must make sure they agree to agree.

3.5 Being right does not mean a complete solution

Having the full support of your team is essential because any solution that is considered appropriate will in most likelihood be incomplete in its original form.

First of all, it will be incomplete in the sense that we will **never** be able to predict every single event that will occur during the implementation of a solution. As every project leader knows, Murphy is the most hyperactive person in the world. Thus, it does not matter how many hours we spend at the drawing board planning to the infinitesimal detail our solution; there will always be something unexpected at the moment of turning our idea into reality.

We do not mean to diminish the need for planning. One thing is to improvise within a plan and a very different one is to improvise the plan. But we must keep in mind that the objective of a plan is not to determine our every action, but rather to determine the route that must be followed and only to determine in principle the necessary actions that ought to be carried out. Only at the moment of facing the actual circumstances is it possible to judge on the most appropriate action to comply with the intended goal.

The execution of every plan will, at many points, demand a certain degree of improvisation to adjust the plan to the specific reality that is encountered. It is only when we count with the total support of the organization that such improvisation can be carried out in favor of the solution in process of being implemented.

When the project does not count with full support, these are the most precious moments for the enemies of the solution. They will have in their hands the possibility of killing the project in one single stroke, and because this will happen in their areas of expertise, they can do it without leaving any trace; or at least none that can be identified by any layman on their subject. These are the moments in which initiatives forced in the organization by senior management find their quiet death.

Another reason why a solution will most of the times be incomplete has to do with what William Dettmer, in his book "Strategic Navigation" (*6) presents as Boyd's Theory of Maneuver Warfare:

> "In much the same way that the presence of even a passive observer influences the observed environment, any action to execute a strategy, however minimal, changes the strategic environment. And, in a changed environment, the original conceived strategy may no longer be optimum".

In other words, the mere fact that we take the first step into the desired change will inevitably alter the system under improvement, which means that all previous analysis will begin to lose validity. Once again, unless we have the full support from the organization to complement our original solution, our project will begin to sink.

As right as a solution can be, it will always need the support of many people to become a success in reality.

3.6 Being right then is, if anything, only the first step of a long journey

In this chapter, we have shared with you our realization that being right is, by no means, a black and white matter. Our perception of what is right is highly influenced by the external circumstances surrounding the particular situation to be analyzed, in as much as it is determined by the moment's conditions of our own internal needs and desires.

We have also discussed the fact that because there are many different angles from which reality is observed and lived by each individual, there is always more than one solution that can be considered "right" for every situation.

Being right then, turns out to be, not as important as we first thought. In order to promote and guide change, there are other elements that are just as important, or more, than having the right solution.

As we discussed in the last chapter, one of those elements is the ability to generate a sense of urgency towards the desired change, while another one, according to this chapter, is the ability to develop full support from the project team and the organization in order to deal with the uncertainties of every implementation process.

After all the importance we had given to being right, accepting its new role as only one of the many elements that are crucial to induce change, is not something that can be easily done. We must warn you that a change of this magnitude cannot be achieved without a great struggle against our already established habits.

However, it is precisely because it is such a difficult change, that we are certain that being able to separate ourselves from the common paradigm of "Being right is enough" is one of the most powerful competitive advantages that any person or organization can develop to face the mighty challenges that are still to come in this wonderful world of ours.

If during your own process of change you feel tempted to give up to the need to always be right, remember that throughout history, the feeling of righteousness has generated more danger and evil than good.

It is a curious phenomenon the one that takes place within ourselves once we develop a sense of being right about something. It is like if a holy truth has just been bestowed on us and henceforward we must fight to death all enemies of this sacred knowledge. We can compare it to those scenes of the Medieval times in which warriors, one knee on the floor and the head bowed, were touched by the sword of their King, giving them by this act the power to wear their armor and use their sword with "honor".

Once we feel sure to be right about something, we make comments and provide testimonies without any regard for their possible consequences. How many times have we used our sword of righteousness to cut in half the smile of satisfaction of someone who put her or his heart and soul on a given task we considered inappropriate? To how many defeated, repented and totally demoralized people have we finished off using the all too right: "I told you so"?

We are living very interesting times. We are witnessing the re-invention of the economic system, most organizations are adopting innovative structures and methods in an attempt to remain competitive, even religions are having to review their long-standing practices. Either we learn to renew ourselves or we will suffer the consequences of staying behind.

We cannot keep on using all our time and energies just aiming to be right and defending that knowledge. We must evolve and move on. Life is not about being right. Life is about loving and caring for our fellow human beings, our world and ourselves. We have spent many years looking for the right answers, it is about time we begin to use the knowledge we have acquired in the process.

Chapter IV. The dilemma behind every problem

"To be or not to be - that is the question:
Whether 'tis nobler in the mind to suffer
The slings and arrows of outrageous fortune,
Or to take arms against a sea of troubles
And by opposing, end them."

- Hamlet

If, as we discussed in the previous chapter, there is always more than one valid solution for every problem, why is it then that so many problems stay with us for so long? How come, even when solutions can be generated abundantly, certain problems are so difficult to get rid of?

Most likely, you, as most people do, have a certain number of problems that have been with you for a while. Some of those problems might even come from many years behind. They may already be considered part of your life, and as such, you do not fight them very strongly any more. But, given the chance, you would welcome the opportunity to solve them once and for all.

Take a few minutes to think about these problems in your life. Are they still alive because you have not been able to think of any solution?

For the vast majority of cases, the answer to the last question is no. Most of the time, our problems keep bothering us not because we do not have a solution, but because solving them generates another problem, one that might be of greater proportions than the one we have right now, or that challenges our most profound principles. Therefore, although we can have more than one solution already at hand, we prefer not to use them because, either we are afraid of the potential risks involved, or we do not know how to implement the solutions in our specific reality without complicating things more. We become trapped in a tug of war.

4.1 Do not give away fake pearls of wisdom

Have you ever known of some employee who, despite his poor performance, remains in the organization or even gets promoted? Or, have you ever heard of a certain client who has not paid his invoices for the last six months, but we still keep shipping new products to him? Why is it that management doesn't just fire the guy or stops shipments to this client?

Let us take an even more dramatic case to illustrate this point: If you do not have a sister, imagine for a moment that you have one, and also assume that she is one of your very best friends. Now, imagine that after what seemed to be a happy marriage for three years, she comes to you for help because her beloved husband, that guy you never really liked, beats her up. What would be your immediate advice to her?

We have presented this very same case to many of our groups and the most frequent answers as to the advice that should be given to this imaginary sister are: leave him!, report him to the police!, hit him back! So, we write down this precious advice and consider it our pearls of wisdom for solving this woman's problem.

Going forward in time in our example, let us further assume that six months later you meet your sister again, and it so happens that she is still married to the same man, and every now and then, he still beats her up. What would be your reaction?

Again, having asked the same question to many different groups, we can tell you that the most frequent reaction is: "Well, we told her what to do, we told her to leave him. But if she is still with him, it is clear that she likes to be beaten up! We cannot help her if that is the case!"

Help her? Do you really think that she needed us to tell her to leave him, report him to the police or hit him back? You can be sure that she thought about those solutions in the first instant that she felt her security threatened. These are indeed what we call "fake pearls of wisdom".

Given a problem, stating the desired situation is not a solution. It is a goal. If a company's sales are down, we cannot go and tell the management of that organization that the solution is to increase sales. That would indeed be the goal. However, the real question is: how?

Then, the fake pearls of wisdom appear: "tell your sales people to increase their efforts"; "use marketing and publicity"; "reduce your prices", etc. Common sense can be such a headache when it comes from well-intentioned people who know close to nothing about our situation!

Presenting the obvious actions, although it might be of help in a very limited number of cases, usually only serves to ignite the fury of the people with the problem, mostly because, without meaning to do it, we are insulting their intelligence.

4.2 Think about what is being gained by tolerating the problem

Although it might sound really weird, before we propose any solution, it is very important to investigate what is currently being gained by tolerating the problem at hand. Yes, you got it right, we are asking you to identify what is being obtained right now by accepting the existence of the problem. Why can we affirm that there is a gain in accepting a problem? Because, if there was nothing to be gained by tolerating this problem, we would have put at end to it a long time ago!

Does this sound totally absurd to you? Think about it very carefully. What has really stopped you from solving a problem for which you already have a solution? Could not it be that, by solving the problem, you would be generating a totally new scenario in which something that you consider important might not be possible anymore?

Let us retake some of the examples we presented before in this chapter: What could possibly be the reason why management does not fire an employee whose performance is clearly unacceptable? It could be that this person knows very well someone who is very important for the company; therefore, although the management of the company knows what should be done, they do not do it because they seek to gain the favor of that person by keeping this employee in the payroll.

Why would we keep shipping new products to a client that owes the company six months worth of payments? The obvious solution would be to stop shipments at once. However, there must be something that is being gained by continuing shipments to this client. It might be that we have an overstock of raw material and the only way to reduce it is by making early shipments before the raw material reaches its expiration date. We can deal with the problem of payments later on.

Finally, what could possibly be gained to make a woman withstand a relationship in which her physical integrity is at risk? The possibilities are many: a father for her children; avoid social ridicule; financial security; to have someone to love; avoid retaliation from her husband; etc.

In Neuro-Linguistic Programming (NLP), this is known as "secondary gains". An example of this is the case of an adult person who has not learned how to drive a car: Driving would provide her or him with the capacity to move in a different way, save time, take charge of certain things and above all, independence of movement. However, her or his secondary gain is to have company every time she or he goes out, which would be lost by learning how to drive a car.

It is also usual to hold that: "every behavior has a positive intention". We just need enough time to figure out the positive intention of this or that behavior. What is important for us at this point is to realize that we tend to use one single way to satisfy our positive intention, even though it could be considered as something undesirable in our life.

Be aware that it does not matter at all whether we think the gain represents or not a fair deal compared with the problem that is being tolerated. What is of real value is to realize that for that particular person, the gain is so important, that she or he is willing to accept the existence of the problem as a means to obtain it.

It may very well be that, given our specific background or upbringing, we either do not feel the need for that specific gain, or that we have found other ways to obtain the same result; and thus, we may consider that this person is tolerating a problem that could be easily avoided.

However, bear in mind that given the very specific experiences, conditions, environment or education of that particular person, there is, in his or her mind, a clear and strong cause and effect connection between the existence of the problem and the satisfaction of what she or he considers a very important need.

You may sustain the principle that every person must add value to the organization and consider irrelevant whether a person is or not the relative of someone important. If that person is under performing, she or he ought to be fired. But, will you really be able to face the consequences of such a decision?

Remember: BEING RIGHT IS NOT ENOUGH!

4.3 The qualifications of a good solution

Many times, what is stopping us to solve a given problem, is not that we do not have a solution, but rather that the solution itself generates a dilemma between solving the problem versus not solving it. Solving the problem, while producing a desired outcome, will generate a new reality that is unknown to us and that could imply risks and consequences that we might not be able to handle. Not solving the problem allows us to remain in a known reality in which we think we can keep satisfying a key need of ours through tolerating the problem.

A good solution then must satisfy at least three conditions: first, it must solve the problem; second, it must make sure that the need that is currently being satisfied through tolerating the undesired problem is not placed at risk; third, it must create options: one way is not an option, two ways create a dilemma, three or more ways offer a basic variety of options from which the person can choose the one that most satisfies her or his vision and needs.

In other words, our solution must break the conflict in which this person or organization has been trapped for a long time.

It is essential to understand that up to the moment in which we pointed our batteries towards a certain problem, the person or organization who suffers from it, has been willing to pay the price of tolerating the existence of such a problem in order to warranty the satisfaction of a certain need that they consider important. For them, the problem is no longer a problem, but a fact of life, a bitter price to be paid for obtaining a strategic gain that they are not willing to lose. Any solution that appears to work against the fulfillment of this gain that has been maintained so far at such a high price, even in the slightest way, will be strongly rejected.

It is of no help to tell a woman to leave her beating husband unless we can also help her find an alternate way to fulfill her need for financial security, companionship, and above all, to avoid retaliation from her husband. We cannot just fire an employee who is in a good standing with an important person for the company without a solid plan as to how we will obtain by another means whatever gain comes from the favor of that person.

Unless our solution can provide these three elements, it will be very difficult to gather the necessary support to implement it at the proper speed.

We can see now why it is that people do not jump immediately into the wagon of just any improvement initiative. Most of us have learned, by tough experiences, that most improvement ideas tend to be only half cooked when they are launched. Unfortunately, many managers and consultants develop projects looking only at the positive effects the initiative will have in the performance of the organization, ignoring completely the side effects that will be generated by losing the strategic gain that is now provided by tolerating the problem, that is part of the conditions in which most of them have become used to living with today.

Most of the times, after an initiative for improvement has been launched, some part of the organization suffers the consequences by losing the means by which they were obtaining a key element to fulfill their functions. Someone will have to go out of her or his way to find a new mechanism to obtain the same results. Some part of the organization will lose the importance or power that comes today to the people who heroically solves the consequences of living with the targeted problem.

Yes, that employee might have been under performing badly, but whenever we were really stuck, he could solve our problem with just a phone call. Yes, that client is late in his payments, but he is the only one who accepts the early shipments that can help us reduce our raw material inventory levels now.

Sometimes, these side effects are nothing but minor bumps in the way of an improvement project. But many times, these are the real obstacles that completely block the advance of the implementation process. We cannot afford to ignore them if we are to move our organizations ahead in fast forward mode.

We must ensure that our solution solves the problem and maintains our strategic gain intact. We have to break the dilemma to avoid having people wishing our projects fail.

4.4 A solution is not a solution unless it fits in reality

Having found a good solution, we then face the challenge of making sure it applies to the specific reality in which it will be implemented.

Some of the most interesting experiences we have lived through as change agents have been related to the automation of a given set of operations or processes within an organization. Usually, our arrival into such projects has been preceded by months of heavy work and even heavier expenditure while attempting to implement the chosen solution.

Most of these kinds of projects tend to incur in big overruns in the budget originally assigned, require far more time and effort than planned, and, to top it all off, fall way short of the expected results.

These kinds of projects are a perfect example of how much managers and consultants can only have eyes for the positive, desirable outcomes, and at the same time, be totally oblivious as to the chain effect of consequences that such projects imply for the day-to-day workings of the organization. The experience ends up being an analogy of us, having to modify our head, in order to make the hat fit.

Please do not misunderstand us. We have nothing against technological solutions. In fact, we ourselves are "technological junkies", always in search of the newest gadget.

We have borne witness that most of the time, the problem is not the technological solutions that are chosen, but the unrealistic expectations about the process of implementation and the possible results of such projects.

The total disregard for the social implications of automating processes or tasks, like the modifications on roles, levels of authority and responsibility that will inevitably come as a consequence of these kinds of initiatives, generates a significant amount of doubt in the organization, enough to bring most projects to a halt.

In today's ultra-competitive markets, most of the implementation plans we have seen for automating any process of an organization are the equivalent of attempting to change a tire of a racing car while it goes at 250 miles per hour and is also having to zig-zag in order to avoid collisions with other cars. It is of little wonder why there are so many crashes and fatal accidents in the process of implementing these projects.

When we point out the impossibility of such plans and we recommend making a better pre-implementation analysis to make sure the current gains obtained from the existing system are clearly identified and secured, and the major impacts on the social system are identified, we are always met by the same answer: "we do not have the time or the budget to do that". So, they start an implementation that will most likely exceed the original time and budget by quite a lot.

And this is only one of the many examples we could provide to show you how much we fail at ensuring that every solution is tailor made for the specific environment and situation in which it will be implemented. We could also talk about cost cutting efforts, re-engineering projects, efficiency improvement programs, and so on.

It seems that there is never enough time to do things properly once, but there is always time to do them two or three times, because we failed on the first attempts.

Failing in the implementation because the solution was not properly adjusted to reality multiplies the original situation of one problem by four: one, we still have the original problem; two, we have wasted the resources we could have used to really fix it; three, we now have a new problem with a solution that does not work as expected; and four, we have lost our credibility with our team.

Tailoring a solution to suit each particular case is an exercise that ought to be carried out with the participation of the key players of the organization. The next chapter (Collaborative Work, The key ingredient) is dedicated to the teamwork required to solidify our original solution.

4.5 Setting up the vision is not a matter of democracy

Make no mistake, making a decision as to what solution ought to be implemented to break the conflict between solving the undesired problem versus maintaining satisfied a certain strategic need through tolerating that problem is the responsibility of no other than the leader of the organization.

She or he is the only person with a wide enough perspective as to determine the full weight of each alternative for the organization as a whole and then decide whether to keep withstanding the problem, as they have been doing so far, or to move ahead and launch an initiative that will inevitably modify the current status quo by bringing in a new solution.

She or he can use any method she or he feels comfortable with to reach her or his decision. They might call for a meeting with their management team, ask for the advice of external consultants, or even read their horoscope in today's newspaper. But the full responsibility for making such a decision lies on the leader.

Actions can be delegated, responsibility can only be shared. As a leader, you are not expected to get involved in the action. Doing so depends on your personal style of leadership. However, you are most certainly expected to be fully accountable for the decision and its consequences.

Joel Barker, in his excellent video "The Power of Vision" (*7) puts it this way:

> A Vision must be:
>
> 1.- Leader initiated.
>
> 2.- Shared and supported by his team.
>
> 3.- Comprehensive & detailed.
>
> 4.- Positive and inspiring.

Therefore, the second duty of the leader, once the vision has been defined, is to share with his team such vision and obtain their support to make it happen. In other words, he must sell his decision to his own organization. Chapter VI. Change selling, is dedicated to this subject in more detail.

4.6 To be or not to be, that cannot be the question any longer

In this chapter, we have discussed a very little known fact about change: most problems stay with us for a long time, not because of lack of solutions, but rather because behind every problem, there is a dilemma which stops us from taking decisive action to solve it. We want to remedy the problem, but its elimination deprives us from a gain that is vital for us. Do we solve it or not? And this question, like in the case of Hamlet, brings all actions a halt.

As a result, we have been able to identify the three critical characteristics of a good solution: it must solve the problem, while at the same time it must maintain the satisfaction of the strategic gain we consider so important as to tolerate it for so long, as well as it must provide options that allow us to feel in control of the solution.

In his book "The Opposable Mind", Roger Martin (*8) offers a clear description of the mental and emotional processes that are needed to generate creative solutions in situations that otherwise would seem to have no other answer than to surrender ourselves to one or the other side of a dilemma:

> "The leaders I have studied share at least one trait, aside from their talent for innovation and long-term business success. They have the predisposition and the capacity to hold two diametrically opposing ideas in their heads. And then, without panicking or simply settling for one alternative or the other, they're able to produce a synthesis that is superior to either opposing idea. Integrative thinking is my term for this process -or more precisely this discipline of consideration and synthesis- that is the hallmark of exceptional businesses and the people who run them"

Another excellent book related to the generation of innovative ideas is "Tools for Dreamers" by Robert W. Dilts and Todd Epstein (*9), while Eli Schragenheim in his book "Management Dilemmas" (*10) presents an specific methodology for solving conflicts.

At this point, it should be said that by no means a good solution must be comprised of one almighty action. Although it is possible to find just one action that can solve the problem and ensure the continued satisfaction of the strategic gain at the same time, we have found that it is precisely the search for this silver bullet that stops most efforts. Like in a chess game, we want to think about all possible implications of every move, while at the same time we attempt to win the game in as few moves as possible.

We have found that it is more practical to break our solution in several components that work together to meet our two defining criteria. For most cases, we tend to use two avenues of solution: one for solving the problem, and another one for keeping the strategic gain satisfied.

What is crucial is that these two elements of the solution generate synergies between each other to ensure that our solution can indeed break the current dilemma. We must avoid seeing these two elements as being two different solutions for two different problems. It ought to be remembered that both elements work towards breaking the same dilemma, and thus, they have to add with each other to this end.

Whatever your decision, you must make one and commit to it. Indecision will get you nowhere.

A final word on conflicts: If you think that finding a solution that meets our two conditions is difficult, we can tell you that it is even more difficult to try to find a way to compromise between the two positions, and that is precisely what we have seen organizations try to do more often than not. That is, if you attempt to find a mediatory position in which you can have the problem solved at certain times, and at others, bring it back to life to meet the requirements of your strategic need, we can assure you that you have just bought your ticket to hell.

Looking for a nice compromise between the two alternatives only keeps the problem alive and accentuates all its negative effects. And worst of all, it sends crossed signals to the whole organization, that will go totally bonkers trying to re-adapt every time to two completely different environments of operation: grow inventories!, now reduce inventories!; be tough with clients!, now be nice to clients!; stop shipments!, now ship as fast as you can!; etc.

Organizations have spent many efforts searching for the operational flexibility that would allow them to switch from one mode of operation to another swiftly, without generating any chaos in their floor shops. However, there is a great difference between becoming flexible and becoming nothing while we attempt to be everything.

Analyze properly the situation; find what is being gained by tolerating the problem you want to solve, develop a solution that breaks the dilemma and make your decision as fast as possible. As you will see in the next chapters, this is only the beginning of a much larger effort, which means we must move at a good pace to achieve the results we want before the situation changes. Following the words of one of our favorite songs by Frank Sinatra: "The best is yet to come"

Chapter V. The Need to Sell Change

"The Matrix is a system, Neo. That system is our enemy. But when you're inside, you look around. What do you see? Businessmen, teachers, lawyers, carpenters. The very minds of the people we are trying to save. But until we do, these people are still a part of that system, and that makes them our enemy. You have to understand; most of these people are not ready to be unplugged. And many of them are so inert, so hopelessly dependent on the system that they will fight to protect it"

- Morpheus
The Matrix

Most of today's leaders see themselves as decision makers, and thus, they tend to focus most of their time and energy on making the best possible decisions. Without them being totally aware of it, they are implicitly working under the assumption that once the best alternative has been found, their organizations will follow suit on its implementation. Through the previous chapters, we have discussed how wrong that assumption can be.

It might be that because the first managerial structures were taken from military experiences, top management does not see the need to convince their staff to follow the established course of action. Some owners even claim that they pay people to follow instructions and are totally opposed to having to spend time selling their decisions to their personnel.

We have come across many ways to justify it, but the fact remains that many leaders fail to see the huge importance of selling their ideas to their own organization.

When it comes to change initiatives, leaders tend to get tired of selling them rather quickly, leaving the enforcement of their ideas, and a systematic elimination of all those who oppose such initiatives, as the most used method to promote their improvement initiatives. And to make matters worse, not only does top management not sell change initiatives appropriately to their people, they even tend to disappear from view for as long as the projects go on.

Leading change does not appear to be one of the favorite activities of top management. It would seem that change projects are such a messy business that organizational leaders prefer to pay as many people as possible to do their dirty work. They call it delegation, and they argue that this is precisely the reason of being for the rest of the organization.

But, it is exactly their commanding presence that these initiatives require more than anything else. So many decisions will have to be made in the spare of the moment while implementing a change project. So many adjustments will be required in the way the organization is structured and things are done, that top management needs to be deeply involved, even devoted, to these initiatives in order to give them a reasonable chance to be successful.

The problem is that these decisions and adjustments will refer mostly to the operational level, the one in which things are actually done on a day-to-day basis. Top management either does not have the inclination to get involved with these matters or does not have the detailed knowledge to make significant contributions on these issues. Thus, in order to avoid getting in the way of the advancement of the project, they prefer to remove themselves from the scene.

They go back to their offices where they do what they do best: analyze the situation of the organization and take decisions to improve it. And so it happens, that while the whole organization is suffering the pains of giving birth to an improvement initiative, top management delivers another marvelous initiative that can indeed contribute significantly to make theirs a better organization.

But, do not worry, surely, this new project will be related to a different area of the organization and will be assigned to a different group of people. Your company can surely manage two change projects in parallel, right?

WRONG! For most organizations, one single change project is more than enough to keep them on their toes while it lasts. We must bear in mind that the day-to-day operations will still have to be dealt with, the normal emergencies and problems will not be stopped, and our competitors will not stay still while we change. And because things will have to be done in new ways, many of our operations will become highly inefficient until our people learn and develop the necessary skills under the new method.

Remember also that in today's organizations, many processes need to travel across several different functions or departments before their completion, which means that changes in any given department will have different degrees of consequences in many others, making one single change an organizational project of tremendous complexity.

Under this light, we do not have to tell you what happens when organizations accumulate more than fifty change projects going on at the same time, which is a common reality for many companies.

It is because of this reasoning that we strongly advocate the idea that instead of going back to their offices to think of new projects, top management must become far more involved in the change projects it launches. They ought to assume the role of change leaders, but more importantly, they must become the heads of internal marketing and sales for their change initiatives.

Selling change internally requires the ability to sell new paradigms and ways of doing things to people at all levels of the organization, but in the same manner, it demands the skills to sell modifications and added components to the original solution to its creators. It is for sure a two-way avenue by which constant trial and error efforts are transmitted and adjusted to ensure that the initiative is well suited to the reality of the organization. Top management is ideally positioned to undertake this coordinating task.

Just as the training of an employee does not end with the welcoming session on her or his first day at work, the selling of change does not end with the kick-off event in which the project is presented to the organization. Change selling is an ongoing task that requires a full perspective of the organizational needs, as well as great sensitivity for its social framework.

5.1 It is all about matching needs with solutions

Selling is, perhaps, the most underrated of the abilities a leader must have. For many people, selling is a gift that you either do or do not have. And what is worse, although selling is the second oldest profession; it is often confused with the first one.

There is nothing more effective to have doors shut in our face than to say "I want to sell you something". Therefore, fear is an integral component of every sale: fear of not making the sale, as well as fear of being sold on something we do not really want.

Unfortunately, as a consequence of all the negative preconceptions related to selling, we all behave in ways that complicate enormously the development of true win-win relationships. As Mahan Khalsa writes in his book "Let's get real, or let's not play" (*11)

> "The bad news is that clients don't consistently get a solution that meets their needs. Even though both of us want it, even though we both lose if it does not happen, both we and the client, engage in counterproductive behaviors."

At the heart of it, selling is all about matching the specific needs of our client with the real attributes of our product or service, so that we can actually call it a win-win relationship.

This implies that every sale must be comprised of at least two main stages: first, finding and developing our client's needs, and second, matching those needs with the characteristics of our product or service.

We found the most powerful insights on matching needs with solutions in the books by Neil Rackham: "SPIN Selling" (*12) and Keith M.

Eades: "The New Solution Selling" (*13). Both make it clear that the key to successful sales is in the proper investigation of the client's needs and their further development to ensure a full view of all its consequences before any solution is offered.

An accurate diagnosis of the need to be satisfied is essential to provide the proper answer. That is a no brainer. Once the need is identified, working further with it to develop a full picture of all the consequences of not fulfilling it is something rarely done. Most people do not see the need to go on this extra mile; we know what the problem is, we have a solution for it, hence, let the bargaining begin.

However, that is precisely the problem. Offering a solution as soon as a need is identified is certainly a very good recipe to receive complaints about the cost of the proposed solution. It does not matter what the price is, it could even be one dollar, and some prospects will still argue that it is too much.

The reason for this is rather simple: we are trying to match a need, valued subjectively in terms of pain or dissatisfaction; with a solution valued quantitatively in dollars. Pain vs. Dollars: This is not good match.

Developing a full picture of all the consequences of not satisfying the identified need is essential to generate a proper perception of the possible value of the proposed solution. Only by matching dollars of consequences vs. dollars of solution can we create a proper match that gives prospects a simple way to evaluate our proposal.

5.2 Basic rules for selling change.

The selling of change has as a primary objective the alignment of the wills and brains in the organization towards the attainment of a specific goal which requires some degree of change in the organization regarding what has become the accepted or normal way of doing things.

People must know what the final goal of the project is to see the sense of carrying on its implementation and, even if they do not fully agree with it, they must be willing to support it to the end.

Like any other sale, the selling of change requires a stage of finding and developing needs followed by the matching of those needs with the elements of our solution. We must identify and develop the particular needs of each person and function within the organization to which we want to sell our project for change and then match them with the particular components of the initiative we have in mind.

Which takes us to the first basic rule for selling change:

Rule#1: No guessing

We cannot assume that, just because we work with someone, we know his or her every need. Nor can we think that knowing the needs of one person, these apply to all those who work in the same department or site. Remember, every person has a different combination of needs, and even for the same person, the priority of needs changes with time. We must do the groundwork and get to know the specific needs of each key person we want to support our project.

Does this sound like a lot a work? Sure, it certainly is. But it is ridiculously less than what will be needed to fix all that will go wrong if we do not do it.

It is certainly much easier to use our power to enforce our decision, at least in the short term. However, forcing an initiative will not secure the real support from our people. Sooner or later, if they are not convinced of the need to implement this idea, they will simply let it die in the fields of the everyday battles.

Rule #2: Sell, sell, sell and sell again.

We have often seen companies spending hundreds of thousands of dollars in a new piece of equipment or software and then, when it comes to training the people who will make use of this new resource, they assume that a one time training of two or three days will be enough for them to learn all that is needed to make this new equipment highly productive.

Unfortunately, this rationale is transferred directly to the selling of change. Most leaders assume that, because they have explained once what the project is about and what is needed from the organization to make it successful, they have done all the selling that is required.

In reality, training and selling of change ought to be done "ad infinitum". We do not think that there is such a thing as "overselling change". The more we repeat the message, the more our organization will understand how serious we are about it, and the more chances there are that we get to transfer the message clearly.

Like in any marketing strategy, you will have to develop a generic message to be used as the "official" communication when you address the whole organization or large groups (your market), and you will also have to tailor specific messages for each function or person (your clients) to make sure you translate it to suit their specific needs or worries.

Make sure you use as many different selling media as is affordable and possible to you. Change the format and wording of your message, and be as basic and simple as possible in your content.

Rule #3: Be consistent

There is nothing more effective to put people off any initiative than inconsistency on the part of top management and the leader of the project. You cannot say one thing and act in a way that goes against what you said. No amount of selling can counter the effect of leaders acting against what has been agreed upon.

So many times we have heard the leader of the project be the first one to complain about his own project. Or, we have seen managers actively fighting a guerrilla war against a project they do not approve of, but do not have the power or arguments to stop.

Crossed signals not only confuse people, but worse than that, they provide the perfect environment for people to do what they please, as they please, and when they please. Because they have a buffet of instructions, they can create their own salad, choosing from all signals the bits and pieces, they need to justify their actions.

How can we fight one of our employees for not delivering a report on time, when the leader of a project for which the general manager requested total support called her or him at the last minute to a "very important" meeting? Of course, he or she did not really care about the meeting, but it gave her or him the perfect excuse for not delivering a report, she or he did not have ready on time.

Management and the leaders of projects must get their acts together, and achieving this, is the total responsibility of top management. It is them who must ensure a proper coordination between the ongoing projects and the day-to-day operations.

Rule #4: Keep the organization informed

Many times a project gets started with a big kick-off event and then nothing more is heard of it. New people are hired, consultants come and go, many meetings are held, but nobody really knows what is going on. The project becomes a kind of foggy presence in the organization. We all know it's there, we feel it, but it's not solid enough for us to know exactly what it is.

And, when there is no official information about something, you know exactly what happens, right? The unofficial channels become overloaded with information. "Radio-gossip" begins its broadcasting services and the organization becomes flooded with all sorts of rumors: "Did you know that the main goal of this project is to make us redundant?"; "Be careful with that consultant, he wants your job"; "I heard that this project was designed to show how bad we are so that the union does not have a strong bargaining position in the coming contract revision"; "A good source told me that the project leader is an alien selecting humans for abduction", etc, etc.

Although we cannot stop gossip from existing, by providing constant information about the development of the project, we can at least make sure that people have the two sides of the coin to consider.

Be sure to inform not only about what has happened, but also about what is to come, so that people are not taken by surprise when a new consultant arrives asking for information about their job, or when a new procedure is implemented.

Above all, be honest in all your communications. Nobody expects a change project to move forward without any disruptions on the way. In any case, you can be sure that all the hick-ups will be the main content of all "radio-gossip" transmissions. Do not give them the exclusive. Allow your organization to learn from all that happens during this constant changing experience. We can assure you that whatever happens in any project, it will not be the last time it comes around.

5.3 Make sure you are really adding value.

Sometimes we are so keen on making the sell that we totally overlook the fact that our solution does not really add value to this particular person or function. Nevertheless, we keep pushing to get some sort of approval that will allow us to move on.

Contrary to what happens in other kinds of sales, when what we are selling is a change initiative, people can say yes without really meaning it, because they will not necessarily have to pay any consequences for letting the project move on. In other words, the money to pay for the consequences of them saying yes, will not come from their own pocket.

So, if we insist enough and we also have some kind of support that stops them from kicking us out of their office, most people will eventually say yes to an initiative they have not really bought into. Besides, most of these kinds of projects will fade away sooner or later anyway, so "get on with it, move away from my computer screen and let me do my regular stuff."

This is precisely how so many projects get started only to be blocked before they get a chance to get to second gear. People let them pass assuming they will die before they are born or very soon afterwards, but when they actually begin to move ahead and changes are starting to create complications in the way things are normally done, there is no lacking of hands willing to hold the killing dagger (Remember Julius Caesar?)

And as a project leader, we tend to be happy to get at least just enough room to get going. So, even though we are completely aware of their silent refusal, we ignore it and get to work on our precious project.

To avoid playing this game, which will most likely end up generating all sorts of problems and even the cancellation of the initiative, we must make sure, we are really adding value to all those concerned with the advancement of our project.

Why should they help us or give us their support if there is nothing for them to gain?, Just because top management says so?, or because it is the right thing to do? Come on! We all know better than that. A sale implies an exchange of goods or services. You have something I want, and I have something you want. If there is not the right balance in this equation, the resulting deal will be sick from the start and sooner or later the illness will be manifest itself in more ways than one.

Sure, every now and then we'll get away with asking special favors from some people who really get nothing by supporting our project. However, change initiatives are such delicate matters that we cannot afford to bring them into the world and let them live on charity. It is our responsibility to ensure their self-sustainability by adding value to the organization and to those who support their development and consolidation.

Chapter VI. Collaborative work, the key ingredient

"Adam Smith needs revision. If we all go for the blond, we block each other, and not a single one of us is gonna get her. So then we go for her friends, but they will all give us the cold shoulder because nobody likes to be second choice. But, what if no one goes for the blond? We don't get in each other's way, and we don't insult the other girls. That is the only way we win, that's the only way we all get laid"

"Adam Smith said that the best result comes from every one in the group doing what is best for himself, right? That's what he said, incomplete ... incomplete, because the best result will come from everyone in the group doing what is best for themselves AND the group"

- John Nash
A Beautiful Mind.

In Chapter IV we established that once a change initiative has been decided upon, the leader has the responsibility of selling it to her or his organization in order to gain their help and support for the implementation process.

The main objective of selling a change project, as we have discussed in the last two chapters, is the alignment of the wills and brains of our people towards the attainment of a very specific goal.

As hard and as lengthy as the selling process can result, its proper execution is vital to create a solid ground on which to build the key element for carrying out change initiatives: Collaborative Work.

You may call it Teamwork, Generation of Synergies, Systemic View, etc. We believe the name is totally irrelevant. What is key for the successful outcome of change initiatives is the added efforts of many individuals who willingly use their unique human talents to achieve a common goal.

No controlling technique or computer program can yet match the amazing capacity of synchronization and adaptation to changing circumstances as human beings who decide to act together as one. When a team comes together as one, we cannot help but to marvel at their performance, feel renewed by their energy, and desire that such happenings were the common experiences in our lives.

One of our favorite examples regarding collaborative work is the story of the Apollo 13 mission. What was meant to be the NASA's third visit to the surface of the moon, became known as a "successful failure" due to the amazing work carried out by the crew and a whole array of people down on Earth solving all sorts of problems to bring the ship and its crew safely back to Earth after an explosion had caused the oxygen tanks to fail.

They had to use the Lunar Module as a "lifeboat" during the return trip because of the damage to the Command Module. They had to face the loss of their main electrical power source and maneuver the ship back to Earth using limited power.

The scenario represented an unknown and dramatic situation to all those involved. However, working as a team, they all contributed their knowledge and experience to turn a disaster into one of the most powerful lessons of human collaboration in history.

Unfortunately, collaborative work, just like being right, has proven so elusive that we tend to think of them more like items of legendary tales than as actual possibilities for our everyday life. Many people have already given up on the possibility and have decided to take a totally egotistical view of life. Some others still believe in it, but doubt that it can become true for them.

This is without a doubt the biggest challenge as change agent: Creating and maintaining alive a true collaborative effort throughout the project. And it is so because, to achieve it, we must gain the real willingness of our people.

6.1 Being many is as important as being right.

The biggest concern for most people regarding a change initiative is: "Will the others do it too?", "Will I not be the only one taking a step forward?", "Is this another flavor of the month idea that will get us nowhere?"

In our experience, the proposed change can be perceived by the members of the organization as right, almost right, dubiously right, or "God only knows", but as long as there is a heavy weight executive pushing it, and a critical mass of key people willing to implement it, most others will embrace it too.

Thus, it is the responsibility of the change leader to make sure she or he fully understands who are the key people that must comprise this critical mass for each specific initiative, for they will be the key to unlock the help and support of the rest of the organization. They will also be the ones that make sure the proper synchronization and adjustments are made on the actual day-to-day operations to ensure the essence of the change initiative is implemented successfully.

Unfortunately, as we have discussed in previous chapters, most leaders are so enthralled in the "being right" paradigm, that instead of selling their initiatives to their own organization, they focus on "convincing" their people about them. They concentrate their energies on showing that this is "the right way to go", gaining more enemies than friends for the initiative as they "defeat" anyone who might think differently.

By enforcing their solution, leaders are virtually eliminating any possibility of support by the critical mass required to gather and guide the help of the rest of the organization. And as a consequence, they are generating a crisis situation from which they themselves will be the most affected victims by becoming slaves of their own decisions and by not getting the results they want.

The first step then towards developing a community in which collaborative work is the norm is getting a community. This might sound too obvious, but we feel the need to make the point very explicit because we have seen a lot of cases in which the leader needs to be the "one-man-band" because they have forgotten to build a community of key people around them.

As a team begins to perform its everyday operations, it is impossible to expect that these will be carried out in a state of full maturity in which every process and product is controlled quantitatively and their continuous improvement is already institutionalized. It is more reasonable to assume that the processes will be rather informal and everyone will be focused on generating some form of output to make the team operational on a very basic level.

It is precisely at this basic level that a sense of community must be developed. It does not matter much if the team is efficient or not at this stage, what matters is that they feel like a team. Two or more people acting as a team, even if this happens under the most rudimentary concepts of teamwork, will eventually outperform the lonely runner with the right solution.

We must remember the words of Voltaire when he said: "The perfect is the enemy of the good". Looking for the perfect answer requires eliminating the good enough solutions, which in most cases would have been the proper way to go. Bear in mind that once we have a good enough solution, developing it further to make it perfect will demand a far greater effort than whatever was needed to have it in its good enough form.

So many things are unknown about what will happen during the implementation of a change initiative, that any added effort towards improving the solution will most likely result in a negligible impact on the actual generation of the desired change.

Get your key members together, develop a good enough sense of community and get going. It is important to understand that a real team is forged through the minute events that happen when we turn our ideas into actions. Most of them will go unnoticed by our consciousness, nevertheless, our brain will be receiving and processing all kinds of signals related to our fellow team members: their behavior, their attitude, their body language, etc. It is then, and only then, that a team comes together as a single unit or cracks as a collection of individuals.

6.2 Is teamwork a reality or just a cliché?

Most people ask this question out of a sense of frustration with their own attempts to make collaborative work part of their everyday lives, either at work or in their own families.

We only have to look at events like the Soccer World Cup, Cirque duSoleil, or any of the Super Bowl half time entertainments to know that the answer to whether teamwork is a reality or not is a resounding yes.

The real question then should be: How do they make it happen? or rather, how can we make it happen?

Striping it to its backbone and working backwards in time, achieving excellence at teamwork requires long and hard practice for which strong discipline is necessary. Discipline needs the establishment of rules. Accepting and following the established rules demands the subordination of every member's will to the team's goal.

So, at the bottom of it all, as the foundational rock of collaborative work is the willingness of each and every one of the team members to subordinate her or his own mind to the team's objective. And this is precisely what makes teamwork such a difficult thing, particularly in these times in which individualism has become the sovereign amongst all human attitudes towards life.

For instance, achieving an effective collaborative work culture requires the sharing of knowledge, resources and responsibilities. This means that although everyone in the team will have a specific function assigned, they cannot be limited or constrained by the performance of such function. They must be willing to alter their role as much as the performance of the team requires them to do so in order to achieve its goal.

Successful teamwork will never happen if the members of the team hoard their knowledge, resources and authority only to be used in the performance of their assigned function. In fact, under these conditions getting any work done is already a miracle.

The first step to give collaborative work a real chance to exist must be taken by the leader of the team, who must be the first one to subordinate her or his mind and personal interests to the team's goal. Her or his willingness to learn with the team as the project evolves, as well as to support the team's decisions, will be the key to shaping the overall attitude towards the project.

She or he will be the target of constant and detailed monitoring from each member of the team, who will be measuring at all times her or his true level of commitment to the team's goal. Her or his every move will be observed and will be subject to interpretation by the team's members. Some of them might even test the leader in different ways before they can really trust her or his motives.

Keith McFarland provides a most powerful example of subordinating the leader's mind and interests to the goal of the team in his book "The Breakthrough Company" (*17)

> "At the end of the American Revolution, the fledging nation was deeply troubled: bankrupt, exhausted by eight years of war, and torn with internal dissension. Some in the military believed that unless they crowned a king, the nation's chances of achieving unity -and survival- were slim. General George Washington was their natural choice. The nation's other founding fathers were a brilliant bunch -Thomas Jefferson, Alexander Hamilton, John Adams, and James Madison- but as a leader, Washington towered above them all. And as the Revolutionary War came to an end, his status was at its apex. As commander-in-chief, he had single-handedly held the revolution together and led a ragtag militia to triumph over the world's greatest military power. But when Washington learned of the plan to crown him

king, he flatly refused the offer. Rather than accepting the crown for himself, Washington insisted on crowning the country. Americans were building a nation that would be bigger than any one person, he believed."

This example allows us to clarify that collaborative work by no means is about sacrificing one's mind and interests for the good of the team. Taking a realistic approach on things, we know that almost no one can be that unselfish all of the time (at least not most people working in business organizations).

True teamwork is about subordinating our mind and interests to the team's goal under the belief that the final outcome will be far better for all involved than anything any member of the team could have achieved by working on their own. It is about working for something far greater and lasting than just generating profits or fame.

If you believe this is too much to ask for on a regular basis, we invite you to attend one of the Jehova's Witnesses District Assemblies anywhere in the world and marvel at the degree of organization they have developed in everything they do. Every single aspect of these events, attended by tens of thousands of people, is taken care of with minute detail, and its execution is flawless.

If you prefer a more mundane example, just visit any of Disney's recreational parks. Every day, they receive thousands of visitors and imprint in every one of them what will be some of the most wonderful memories of their lives.

The common factor in these examples is that in both cases, every single one of the members of these organizations has decided to subordinate her or himself to their organization's goal. Not out of personal sacrifice, or because there are no other options. They do so happily because they strongly believe that achieving the goal of their organizations is far more important and will provide them with far more satisfaction towards achieving their personal goals than anything they can achieve on their own.

So, is teamwork a reality? You can bet on it, provided you can first submit your own mind and interests to the goal of your team.

Now, the remaining question is: Are you willing to do just that?

6.3 Move at the speed of the slowest resource

If you can create a basic team of key people and if you can instill in them the desire to subordinate their performance to the attainment of the team's goal, you will be well on your way towards generating an effective collaborative work culture.

The third element required to ensure a basic tripod on the base of this working structure, is a pragmatic philosophy for the administration of the team's resources. A way to ensure that at every moment the key members' attention is focused on the tasks that will benefit the most the team's performance.

Our research showed that there is no better philosophy to make managerial decisions than the Theory of Constraints presented by Dr. Eli Goldratt in his book "The Goal" (*18).

At the core of this school of managerial thought is the fact that the overall performance of every system, regardless of how big or complex it might be, is determined by one, or very few, constraining factors. Thus, top management must always be on the lookout for these constraining factors and then use them as the pivoting point for all their management decisions.

The whole team must subordinate their performance to the achievement of the maximum possible outcome from the constraining resource. In other words, the whole team must move at the speed of the slowest resource, the system's constraint.

Many people interpret this as a waste of resources and a cause for underperformance of the whole team. But think about it carefully.

What does really happen when every resource in your team works as hard and as fast as they can regardless of how the others are doing?

Eventually, at least one element of the system will not be able to keep up the pace, generating a chain reaction that will bring to a halt, one by one, all of the other resources. Just look at what has happened to the global economy because the whole world spent and committed money faster than we were really generating it.

Under the collaborative work culture, subordinating the performance of each member to the speed of the slowest resource means that every resource of the team will perform their functions as fast and well as they possibly can and then, when they are done, they must use their remaining capacity to find ways to help (directly or indirectly) to improve the performance of the constraining resource.

Many times, after the whole team has made whatever changes were necessary to improve the performance of the slowest resource, a different element will become the constraining factor for the overall performance of the system. When this happens, the whole team must realign the subordination of their performance to maximize the output of the new constraint.

Following the pace of the constraining resource will ensure the best possible return on all investments made by the team in terms of achieving the established goal.

6.4 When you have a team, you can be right even when you are wrong

Having surrounded yourself by a team of key people who are willing to subordinate their performance to the team's goal, and managing your team based on the philosophy of concentrating your key resources on the factor that limits the overall performance of the team, you would have set the basic environment for the emergence of a collaborative work culture.

Of course, this is only the beginning. The establishment of rules, the development of a working discipline, and the ensuing hard work needed to make collaborative work flourish and sustain itself are still to be implemented. These aspects that will be dealt with in the next chapter: "Change Management, the Necessary Companion to Execution".

But, just by laying down the foundation properly, you will start to see the fruits of collaborative work soon enough. Small successes will become the regular fuel propelling your team to achieve more and better results as time goes by. Your team members, in order to maximize their performance and make efficient use of the available resources, will develop new and surprising ways of communication. A very unique microcosm of activity will become alive before your very eyes.

To most outsiders, the sight of a team working hard under a collaborative philosophy, might give them the impression of total chaos. Things will be happening in ways that result difficult to understand by people who are not deeply involved with the team. Shouts, hand signals, eyebrow lifts, all have a well defined meaning for those involved and are an essential part of a wonderful symphony of people in collaborative movement.

And do not believe even for a second that just because a team has achieved a certain level of collaborative work everything will go on smoothly from then on. You can be sure that even for these well synchronized teams, many things do not happen as expected and many mistakes are made along the way.

But that is perhaps one of the most fascinating aspects of real teamwork. Even though things will go wrong at many points, the team itself will develop the ability to adjust its performance to overcome whatever problems come around, making it look to the untrained eye like if there had been no problem at all. This is why we can tell you that when you have a team, you can be right even when you are wrong.

If you ever want to witness this magic, get a seat behind the scenes of a theater play, at the kitchen of a popular restaurant or at any manufacturing site one day before the company President's visit.

6.5 When the leader becomes the constraint

Unfortunately, despite its many advantages, collaborative work is yet to make it to the top ten favorite management tools. And the main reason for this is that collaborative work requires leaders to play a completely different role from the one that has been accepted for many years.

By attempting to make every decision, control every move and claim credit for every small success, the leader institutes her or himself as the constraint of the system.

We have seen it happen many times in many different organizations and environments: As the team begins to develop, the leader, who still wants to rule under the "being right is enough" paradigm, becomes ever increasingly the limiting factor for the performance of the team.

Mostly, this happens because leaders still see themselves as a separate entity "on top" of the team, instead of being one with the team. This mental separation into two entities, the working and the ruling class of the team, blocks the leader from becoming fully functional at the speed and rhythm of the rest of the team.

In our experience, the sole concept of the leader being one with the team has proven to be by itself a strong reason to make many top managers consider collaborative work as a repulsive socialist tool that ought to be banned from existence. They immediately see a threat to their status quo and to the position they have fought so hard to obtain.

However, being one with the team does not at all mean that the role of leader is no longer necessary. Our experience has shown time and again that most attempts to bring democracy into the work place usually end up in anarchy and total chaos.

Being one with the team means that in order for the leader to fully understand the inner workings of her or his team, and thus, to better lead it, the leader must see her or himself as one more resource at the team's disposal.

We have already established that the leader must be the first one to subordinate his or her own interests to the team's goal. But to be one with his or her team, the leader has to go beyond that. The leader has to also share and subordinate her or his knowledge, experience, contacts, strategic vision, etc. to the team's goal. In short, she or he must surrender to the good of the team all that makes her or him a leader.

The typical reaction to this statement is: "If I surrender all that makes me the leader to the team's good, what would I have left?, couldn't anyone be the leader then?, doesn't that make me unnecessary?" Many leaders are afraid to be seen as one more member of the team because it makes them look human. Everyone can see them, touch them and realize that they also make mistakes. In short, they become vulnerable.

The answer to what you will have after you have surrendered all your leader powers to the team is rather simple: ALL YOUR LEADER POWERS. The fact that you place your leading powers at the service of the team does not at all mean that you will be stripped from them. To make use of them, the team has to do so THROUGH you.

As to the whether anyone can be the leader when you submit your leader powers to the team's goal, the answer is yes, and that is precisely the point. The fact that you are the leader does not necessarily mean that you can effectively lead your team through every possible situation. Nor does it mean that by sharing the leadership you won't still be the leader at the end of the day.

Allowing the members of your team to take leadership as the situations require will not only propel your team to better and faster results, but will also augment their respect for you as their leader. This will also empower them to become better team members once they feel in their own skin the complexities of leadership.

Finally, as to the matter of your possible redundancy as their leader once they know all your tricks and have made use of your leadership power, we must tell you that the real answer is completely in your own hands.

On the one hand, nobody can really warranty that you will keep your position of leader, not your boss, not Corporate head quarters, not even the CEO of your company. In these uncertain times for most of the world's economies, even they must be wondering whether their own positions are at risk.

Curiously enough, our experience has shown that what really bonds leaders with their teams is the recognition that despite their humanity, they are always willing to overcome their own weaknesses and try again when most people would rather give up. It is their relentless search for the common well being that makes them irresistible to follow and support.

The only way to generate some kind of assurance for your current position as leader is to keep adding value to your organization, your team and yourself. And as the leader of a collaborative team, this means that you must be constantly learning new tricks, constantly proving you are the best leader the team can have, and also constantly proving to yourself that you have done the best you can.

Chapter VII. Collaborative Selling of Change

> *"The colossal misunderstanding of our time is the assumption that insight will work with people who are unmotivated to change. Communication does not depend on syntax, or eloquence, or rhetoric, or articulation but on the emotional context in which the message is being heard. People can only hear you when they are moving toward you, and they are not likely to when your words are pursuing them. Even the choicest words lose their power when they are used to overpower. Attitudes are the real figures of speech"*
> *- Edwin H. Friedman*

A great number of the CEOs, Presidents, General Directors and Owners of Businesses with whom we have talked, admit that at some point of their careers they have seriously considered the need to involve their teams more deeply in the change processes that ought to be carried out during the life of an organization.

Therefore, in one way or another, they have already attempted to sell their ideas or decisions to their personnel. Unfortunately, in most cases, the resulting experiences have not been that positive. The results have varied from total confusion among their staff to clear insubordination movements against them.

It is not surprising then, that the idea of "selling" their change projects to their own personnel is not a fundamental principle shared by the top leaders of most organizations.

After a detailed analysis of the experiences that have been told to us, as well as the existing literature on the subject, we noticed that even though the subject of transferring ownership of change projects to the key people is accepted, in principle, as a logical element of good leadership, very little exists that shows "how" to achieve it.

Because of this, those who actually put into practice this key aspect of collaborative leadership tend to do so without a proven method, and thus, they do it fundamentally based only on their intuition and good judgment.

Having participated in the implementation of a fair number of change projects, we have encountered time and again an evolutionary series of stages that must be dealt with one at a time, like peeling an onion, as we move forward with our projects.

These stages have given birth to a very specific process which has proven to be very effective; particularly, because it allows us to focus our energy in achieving very concrete elements that are conductive to making the final sale, rather than attempting to accomplish the sale in one big step, which can turn out to be too difficult to manage from the very beginning.

This sequence of stages allows our teams to better understand and assimilate each element of the change process, as well as the desired overall change, as we move along the process. This is truly useful for many leaders since one of the most frequent problems we must face when guiding an organization or project, is that because our teams are so focused on the everyday operations, they constantly lose sight of the overall goal of the business or project.

This collaborative selling process consists of the following steps:

7.1 Step#1: Create a collaborative environment for the sale

Let us make it very clear from the beginning: in order to achieve a successful sale we need the active collaboration of the person, or persons, who will do the buying. Any other thing would be an imposition or a sham, but not a sale.

For starters, we, the ones doing the selling, must avoid at all costs thinking that because we have a solution that seems plausible (i.e. "Being right"), we have the strongest bargaining position in the selling process. As we have discussed at length in this book, being right is not enough to get other people to respect us and follow our instructions.

In fact, being right not only doesn't give us a stronger position in the selling process, but rather the opposite. Since we have already analyzed the situation and found a possible solution, we now see how things could be better if the solution were implemented. As a result, we want something from the people doing the buying (help us perform the change), while the people doing the buying do not want anything from us.

We have come across some leaders and consultants who believe that the less their people know about the solution that is to be implemented, the better, because in that way they cannot ruin it. Therefore, although they call the process of transferring the solution to their people as the "buy-in" process, in reality, what they are attempting is only to overcome their people's resistance to do what they have already decided is best for everyone.

This "buy-in" concept implies that we, the developers of the solution, must get the people whose help we need to implement the solution, to buy into performing an active role in the implementation process. We find this idea very similar to the attitude taken by parents when having to give medicine to their children: "Here is the pill, and whatever means I use to make you swallow it are for your own good"

Creating a collaborative environment for the sale implies that rather than making our teams swallow our pre-conceived solution, we must be willing to share with them the development of the final solution that is to be implemented, which can take a very different form than the one we had originally thought of.

In other words, we will both be buying and we will both be selling: We will be selling our view of the problem, our experience during the original analysis and our initial idea for a solution; while they will be selling their own view of the problem, their experience with it, and their opinions regarding our proposed solution.

Unless we are willing to buy from them some of their arguments, and modify the proposed solution accordingly, they will not buy into becoming an active part of its execution.

The problem is that many times, as change agents or project leaders, we do not have the power to buy into their objections. Even as leaders of the organization, sometimes we are powerless to face the attitudes or arguments presented by our people and thus are unable to engage them into any kind of collaborative effort.

If that is the case, it would seem that we have to make a fundamental decision which involves two basic alternatives: should we go around this person and move on with the project?, or should we call the project off?

This is one of the most hated situations for most of the change agents we know. They argue, that managing a change initiative should not have to be further complicated by the personal problems and quarrels between the people in the organization.

Well, we believe that whoever thinks that way, does not truly understand the role of a change agent. Being a change agent has everything to do with identifying and solving the personal problems and quarrels between the people in the organization in order to move forward a given initiative. Why else should organizations need change agents?

Change will always involve personal issues. So, being a change agent is all about developing personal relationships with the people involved. There is no way around it.

Thus, creating a collaborative environment for selling change is all about developing the personal relationships with the people whose help and support we need to make the desired change happen.

Nowadays, when we meet new people, and they ask us what do we do, we like to start the conversation by answering: "We are organizational therapists". Although this answer started as an internal joke regarding the many hours we spent dealing with personal issues in our projects, we now understand that this answer is far closer to reality than any other description we could have come up with.

7.2 Step#2: Identify the key people to whom you must sell the change

As we discussed in the previous chapter, the proposed change can be perceived in many different ways by the members of the organization, but as long as there is someone "high above" sponsoring it, and a critical mass of key people willing to implement it, the rest of the organization will follow suit.

Thus, it is vital to identify who are the key people forming this critical mass for each change initiative, for they will be the key to unlocking the help and support of the rest of the organization.

This group of people varies tremendously from one organization to another, as well as from one change initiative to another.

It would sound obvious to say that we are looking for the people who can "pull" and align other people and resources to support our change effort. However, it is not always that obvious what kind of "pull" or alignment is needed for each project.

We must ask ourselves: "For this specific change initiative do we need the rebels in the organization or the conservatives?"; "Can we take it slowly or would we have to roll it over all opposition?"; "Do we need the brains of the corporation or the muscle?"

It is essential to fully understand what kind of pull is needed for your project in order to gather the proper mix of key people around your specific initiative.

Take into account that besides selling your change initiative to the people from whom you will need help and support, you must also sell it to those people in the organization that could slow it down or even block it. Many times, all you need from certain key people in the organization is for them to do nothing at all with regard to your project. In other words, to let it be.

Whatever the combination of key people required to move forward your initiative, there could be no doubt that in every project, all the members of Top Management must be targeted by your selling strategy. Every single one of them has the power to help or block your initiative by all kinds of methods.

7.3 Step#3: Create a sense of urgency

In Chapter II, we established the need to create a sense of urgency in our change efforts. During the collaborative selling of the change, this sense of urgency will become essential to avoid people sitting on the fence looking calmly at all the movement around them, but taking no decision regarding their position about the proposed change.

You must make sure that at every step, people perceive the need to make up their mind with regard to your change proposal. Are they in or are they out? Will they help or not? They must declare themselves, one way or another, as soon as possible. There is little more complicated for a change agent than having to deal with people who try to play on both sides of the field.

Developing the burning platform scenario described in Chapter II will be of tremendous help to push people towards taking a definite stand in favor of our change initiative.

It is important to mention that we should not confuse instilling a sense of urgency about our change initiative with doing everything about our project in a rush. Developing a sense of urgency is not about cutting corners or dong things half way. It is a mental framework about the importance of doing things as soon as possible to avoid any sort of procrastination. It is about facing whatever difficulties or problems we must face as soon as possible to deal with them and get them out of our way in the best possible manner, instead of doing it in the last possible minute using all sorts of improvised measures.

7.4 Step#4: Demonstrate the existence of the problem

It is usually the case that as we start a new change project, the participants tend to deny the existence of any kind of problems in their areas of responsibility. The higher the rank, the more they will argue about the holiness of their sanctuaries. As leaders, we cannot assume that, because we see a problem, other people will see it too.

It usually takes some time and questioning before they are ready to talk about their problems. And when they eventually begin to accept the fallibility of their areas, they tend to start by explaining that whatever problem they might have is someone else's fault.

Thus, our first step in selling the change internally must be to demonstrate the existence of the problem we want to solve. Do not bother talking about possible solutions, if our internal clients do not see the problem, or if they think that it is not their problem, any solution presented to them, regardless of how brilliant it is, would seem absurd and costly. Rather than embracing change, they will actively oppose it, since it will only disrupt their current status quo.

That is why, when it comes to promoting and guiding change, the expressions "there is no problem" and "it is not my problem" should be feared as if they were the plague. We must fight them will all our might and produce enough evidence, preferably physical, to demonstrate that the problem is there, and why it is a problem.

"Trust me", "believe me", "I am telling you" are not arguments that we can use to convince our personnel about the existence of a problem. Even if we are in a position of high trust or power, we cannot base the entire sale on their faith or fear of us.

This is a critical point for the following stages, because it will be the anchor of all future arguments. She or he must not only agree with us about the existence of the problem, she or he must be totally convinced of its existence.

7.5 Step#5: Demonstrate the specific consequences of the problem on your client

Once we have managed to make our key personnel see the problem as we do, the next stage of the sale implies identifying the specific impacts of that problem on them or on their work.

Many times, once we have demonstrated the existence of a problem, the typical reaction is something like: "oh, yes, it is true, we have that problem, but that is not really MY problem"

By "that is not really my problem" they mean one of two things: either the problem we have just mentioned exists but it has no negative effects on them, or they do not even care about whether that problem has any impact on them because there is another problem that is far more urgent for them to solve.

In any case, finding out the consequences of the targeted problem for every specific person we need to sell the idea of supporting our solution is the only way to create a win-win scenario for developing a true collaborative relationship.

The kind of help and support we get from every person will be directly related to the amount and seriousness of the consequences we can find and demonstrate between the problem we want to solve and that person.

Our favorite way to develop this network of consequences coming out of the targeted problem, are logic trees and mind mapping techniques.

For more detailed information on logic tress we highly recommend the books, "Breaking Constraints to Achieve World Class Performance" by William M. Dettmer(*14), and "Thinking for a Change" by Lisa J. Scheinkopf (*15)

On mind mapping, "The Mind Map Book", by Tony Buzan (*16) is a great source. You can also start using Mind Maps immediately by acquiring the software Mind Manager at www.mindjet.com. This is a great and friendly tool to develop connections between a central topic and as many consequences of first, second or more levels as needed without getting all tangled up.

7.6 Step#6: Demonstrate the possibility of solving the problem

The next stage for the internal selling of a change project is to demonstrate to our personnel that the problem we have brought forward does have possible solutions that work.

It is very often the case that once we have successfully demonstrated to the group the existence of a problem and its consequences on their own life, we get to hear something like: "yes, we do have that problem, and now that you put it that way, we agree that it is also our problem, but it is not really new; that problem has been there for a long time and there is nothing that can be done to fix it. It is impossible to be solved".

This is such a dangerous statement. We have come to consider it the most terrible serial killer of change initiatives. Most people stop dead at the mere suspicion of facing an impossibility.

To back up their claim, people use arguments like: "we tried to solve it in the past, but nothing good came from such effort"; "we have done some benchmarking, and many competitors have the same problem"; "that is the way your father is, so we have to live with it".

In other words, we often prefer to bang our heads against a well-known problem, rather than risk banging our heads attempting a solution we consider impossible. We adapt so well to our circumstances that we even invent special helmets in order to endure our regular doses of head banging against our well-known problems.

Would you buy a solution for a problem you consider impossible to solve? Of course not! Thus, it is our duty, if we want to make the internal sale, to show our team that our problem might be very difficult to solve, but not impossible.

Allow us to share with you a family story to illustrate this point. After living five years in our house, the light bulb at the top of the stairs stopped working. Because we did not have a proper ladder to climb all the way to the squared hole in the roof where this bulb was located, we decided to leave it like that until we had the time to buy a proper ladder. Since this was not a priority in the family schedule, you can easily imagine that several months went by and the bulb remained unchanged. We became so used to that light not working, that we came to consider it "normal" in our everyday lives.

Things would probably have stayed that way until this day had it not been for our six-year-old daughter. One night, as she was climbing down the stairs to get a glass of milk from the kitchen, she fell. Nothing serious happened to her, but her fall gave us the sense of urgency we needed to face the amazing challenge of changing the light bulb.

No, of course we did not buy the proper ladder. However, the next morning, right after breakfast, we started to pile objects on top of each other in an attempt to reach the ceiling above the stairs' recess. We built the most unstable structure you can imagine: A table, two chair, a tall stool, some books. But still, the bulb was unreachable. We were about to give up, when our daughter, who had been witnessing with great delight the construction show from one of the steps, said: "why don't you change it from above?" ...

The concept of "out of the box solution" could never have been more rightly applied. We had been trying to reach the bulb from the inside, when the simplest solution was to climb to the roof using the stairway that was already built in the house, and reach it from the outside. It had seemed like such an impossible task a few minutes before and now it was so simple.

The problem with the expression "it is impossible to solve" is that we tend to use it far too lightly. Yes, obviously there are some things that can be considered impossible and most of them because we have not been able to figure them out yet. But, human history is full of examples of how through the cumulative knowledge of many people, things that were considered impossible in other times, are later on everyday realities; like airplane traveling, cell phones, internet and digital photography.

In our work promoting and guiding change projects, we have come to realize that when people say that something is impossible in everyday mundane activities, they are not referring to these kinds of masterly feats. Mostly, people use the expression "it is impossible to solve" when what they should really be saying is "I do not know how to solve it, and I do not really want to take the trouble to know how to solve it, because then I will have to do something about it".

How many times have you seen a person react only when they have lost something that is of great value to them? How often do we give in to our comfort and status quo and prefer to label things as impossible in order to avoid having to do something about them?

It is only when we are pushed to the very limit by external circumstances that we are willing to face and overcome the impossibilities in our lives. It is only when we are at the edge of the abyss that our creative mechanisms get a jump start and suddenly, as if inspired by divine intervention, we are able to identify possible avenues of solution were before there was none.

This is perhaps the most difficult stage of the whole collaborative selling of change process. Many times, in order for our personnel to accept that a certain problem can indeed be solved and be willing to cooperate in the development of its solution, we will have to take them to the very limit or wait for an eternity for them to get there on their own.

This is a very delicate moment because there are no clear rules as to which is the best way in this crossroads: Force the situation or wait for the team to get on their own. In practice, we try to do both.

If we must, we force the solution a bit and then we analyze the reaction from our team very carefully. We push, we explain, and then we wait for the team to assimilate the change. Once the team is with us again, we force the solution a little more and we continue this way until the key personnel breaks their stationary inertia and begins to move on its own.

It is vital to realize that the above mechanism can only be used to break a rooted passive cultural paradigm in our personnel. We should resist our Lone Ranger instincts by all means, and should not attempt to go forward without our client having bought in her or his role as an active part of the solution.

If they are willing to go along, but still see the solution as our responsibility, we must go back as many stages of the sale as needed until we are able to make them realize the importance of taking a proactive stand towards solving the problem.

What happens then if our problem is not really impossible to solve? What if the solution implies less head banging than our current regular doses? What if we were to show you many examples of how other people have already solved that very same problem?

7.7 Step#7: Work with your internal client on tailoring the solution to her or his reality

We know the answer to the last question, we have heard it many, many times: "Well yes, you are right, that sounds like a possible solution. But we are so different from them that we cannot see how your solution can help us. That is not our case."

There is a catch-22 that is very often presented to us as change agents: As part of the natural process of getting to know us before they can trust us with their improvement initiatives, many prospects request a list of references and -or- a list of the projects in which we have worked on. Regardless of how long and varied the list we provide is, nine times out of ten, they will come up with an argument that will sound like this: "Very impressive, but, haven't you worked with someone more like us?"

What makes it a catch-22 is the fact that by "us" they really mean "them", and being a prospect, of course we have never worked with "them" before. Even if we have as a reference a sister organization, their own corporate offices, or any company in the same industry, the fact is that every person and organization considers her or his situation unique and more complex than any other.

Whenever we present an example of how other people or organizations have already solved the very same problem they have just described, they proceed to give a detailed demonstration of how their situation differs from the example provided: "... The Germans?, of course they have solved it, they are so organized and disciplined, but look at my team, if only I could make them get to the meetings on time at least once"; "Yes, my neighbor had this problem before, but I do not have a father with the same influence as his"; "Well, of course my brother is getting better grades than me, he has no life other than school!"

This seems like a very safe position for somebody who does not want to do any buying-in, since it would be practically impossible to find another person or organization with exactly the same circumstances as the ones they have. Thus they can maintain their belief that in their case, the problem is impossible to be solved. They get their helmets back on and resume banging their heads a million times more against their very familiar problems.

This stage of the sell requires a great deal of empathy in order to be able to fully understand the nuances that make this situation so unique according to the perspective of our key personnel. We must pay a great deal of attention to all the arguments they present and then, instead of refuting each argument, make sure that the solution is adapted to deal with each and every one of those issues.

Please note that up to this step, we have presented stages that require some degree of preparation before we show ourselves before our team members, that is why all the previous steps started by saying "Demonstrate ...". This, and all the coming steps, start with "Work with your internal client on ...", meaning that from here on, the sale becomes a collaborative effort.

As stated in the previous step, at this stage, your client must be willing to bring forward her or his knowledge of the problem, while you provide your knowledge of the solution. It is only by working from both ends that the proper tailoring can be done to make sure that the solution applies to this specific case.

Furthermore, be aware that in this step, all we are aiming to do is to sell the applicability of the solution to this particular case. Work with your team only on those issues that will make the solution fit in this environment.

7.8 Step#8: Work with your internal client on a plan to solve all possible obstacles

Returning to the general evolution of selling improvement projects internally, at this point, we have already shown the existence of the problem to be solved, we have demonstrated the negative effects of this problem and we have proved that it is possible to solve it by working with our key personnel on those issues that make this a special application of the solution. We now face one of the final barriers to change: "YES ... but".

Being engineers, we tend to fall in love with the cleverness of the solutions we develop with our internal clients. We sometimes even joke among ourselves about winning the Nobel Prize for the brilliant analysis and solution we came up with. You can imagine then that there was nothing more infuriating to us than to finish such a solution only to be met by a long list of "yes ... but".

Originally, it was thought that this problem was impossible to be solved, and now that we have developed together some avenues of solution, instead of immediately promoting our names in the list of candidates to obtain the Nobel Prize, our personnel gives us a series of big and resounding BUTs. All they do is present huge obstacles that are in the way of reaching the final solution. "Yes, that is a possible solution, but we do not have the amount of money that is needed"; "Yes, we could do that if only we had some more personnel"; "Yes, that would work, but corporate would never give their support."

What is the matter with these people? Why can't they see that all they are bringing up are silly excuses compared with the cleverness of the proposed solution?

Well, it took some really heavy duty head banging on our part to understand that when people react by saying "yes ... But", all they are really doing is asking for help in the process of tailoring in more detail the proposed solution to their specific reality.

We can now share the good news with you. Whenever you reach this point, you have already overcome the most difficult barriers for change. Up to this point, we had been dealing with emotions, perceptions and beliefs, all of which reside in our minds. Reaching the "yes ... But" barrier, means that you have been able to shake and break the spider webs in your mind and are now ready to face the real world, mainly physical, challenges. Which means it is time to get our hands and feet to join our brain into the action.

Unfortunately, we have noticed that, for some reason, this is precisely the point where those who have promoted and guided the change initiative up to this point, either as top management of the organization or as external consultants, commit the most outrageous act: they leave the detailed tailoring of the solution and its implementation totally in the hands of their teams.

Perhaps, they do so because they minimize the obstacles presented by the organization's personnel, or perhaps they do it because they are too exhausted after creating such a clever solution. Whatever the reason, the fact remains that instead of pushing forward to ensure that the tailoring and the implementation are done without damaging the essence of the solution, they turn and abandon the project as if their work had been done.

We consider this an outrageous act not because the teams do not have the skills or brains to carry it forward. The fact that they have them goes without questioning. It is because the process of tailoring the solution and the process of implementing it are so delicate, so fragile beneath the constant pressure of the day-to-day operations, that many projects will die before they are even born after losing a top leader who protects them and gives confidence to the personnel involved with them. Or even worse, they will be conceived with genetic deformities that will eventually cause their death.

Tailoring and implementing the solution require as much care and nurturing, as a newborn baby requires from all her or his family. Conceiving a baby requires passion and then a period of careful gestation. But we all know that the task of parenthood does not end when the baby is brought into this world. We know too well that parenting will become a full time job for many years thereafter.

Because of this, parenting can become a very stressful job if done only by the parents. Also because we are so blind to our own bad habits, we cannot help but transfer them to our kids who will most likely adopt and perfect them to our total dismay.

Having people around to help us raise our children, despite the potential for a different form of stress, gives us the opportunity to make it a more enjoyable experience and provides our kids with more points of view to better understand and deal with life. That is why in Africa, there is a proverb that says: "It takes a village to raise a child".

Exactly the same applies to improvement initiatives. Although most teams can do a very good job of tailoring and implementing solutions on their own, having an internal leader from the top level, as well as external help, particularly the people who developed the original solution, will significantly increase the chances of success of their improvement initiatives.

It is also during this process that we become aware of the real relevancy of our solution for the organization. In some cases, we will discover that the solution we generated is not totally appropriate given the specific issues that must be considered in this particular case.

In our experience, facing this situation openly with our internal clients generates a higher level of trust in us, so even though we might not get to sell the specific solution we had already developed, it is highly probable that they will want to keep working with us in the development of alternate solutions.

If this is the case, by having shown our key personnel honesty in our professional behavior, we would have achieved the greatest sell of all, because we would have provided evidence of our unshakable professional ethics, and that is the most valuable asset a change agent can have.

7.9 Step#9: Work with your internal client to create a team capable of implementing the plan

If all the previous steps have been carried out diligently, by now you ought to have internal clients who are very motivated and looking forward to getting the plan in action. And it is only natural to think that you would also be more than willing to move forward. In fact, it is very likely that you will now be under pressure from your internal clients to start moving.

There is one final step in the collaborative selling of change process which must be carried out carefully before heading into the real action: we must sell to the organization the need to create a "dream team" for the project.

Why do we need a "dream team"? Because after all the work we have done to get to this point, we would hate to see our project being handed down to the most incapable team to perform it, right? Unfortunately, that is what happens in most cases.

When the time comes to assign resources to these projects, particularly people, there is a great tendency to assign the people "we can afford to lose". In other words, we do not give these initiatives to the most capable people in the organization, but rather to those that can be spared from the day-to-day operations.

By doing this, a game between two factions is generated within the organization: the home team, represented by the most experienced people, defending the way everyday operations have been carried out until now, against the newbies team, formed by young and inexperienced guys who attempt to score a goal by changing some of the current ways to do things. Which team do you think has the most probabilities of winning?

And do not accept for a second the argument that "we will give you the best resources as tutors for the project on a part time basis." This only means that you will never have them when you need them. Either you have them or you do not, and that must be clear from the start.

If an ideal team cannot be afforded because there are more impending issues in progress, it is better to wait until those matters have been resolved and the right personnel can be assigned to the project.

Your objective in this step of the sale is to make sure the organization sees the need to form the best team possible to manage this project and also that it is willing to work with you in finding the best alternatives to do so as soon as possible.

7.10 WARNING! Do not jump any step!

Do take note of all the stages that had to be overcome and all the effort that was needed before we could get to the physical action stage. It is of the utmost importance that you become aware of these steps and the need to walk through them systematically, especially when it comes to guiding team efforts.

What is the point of jumping straight ahead into action when at the back of your mind you think the solution is impossible? Or if one or more of your key team members believe that the solution does not apply to them?

Recently we had the opportunity to visit one of the wonders of the engineering world: the Hoover Dam in the border between Nevada and

Arizona in the USA. It is indeed a marvelous technological feat, and when completed in 1935, it was both the world's largest electric power generating station and the world's largest concrete structure. Many impossibilities and huge obstacles had to be overcome in order to build such a colossal structure.

Two pieces of information about this marvel are of particular relevance with regard to our discussion. The first one is that according to the official information, its construction started in 1931 and was completed in 1935, more than two years ahead of schedule. The second one is the fact that it took almost 10 years of previous negotiations between the States that would benefit from its construction and the Federal Government to finally reach an agreement amongst them and gain Congressional approval for the construction of the Dam.

Ten years of negotiations were followed by three years of architectural and engineering wonders. Can you start to see now why we claim that being right is not enough?

It does not matter how right your idea or solution is, all that is required to sabotage it is one member of your team, one fiber of your mind thinking that the idea is impossible to make it so.

We must do the necessary work to overcome each and every one of the stages of the proposed collaborative selling of change process before we put our ideas into action.

Chapter VIII. Change models, the complement to execution

"Just as a multitude of laws often creates excuses for vices, so that the best regulated state is that which, having very few laws, makes those few strictly observed, instead of the great number or precepts which make up logic, I thought that the four following precepts would suffice, provided that I could make a firm, steadfast resolution not to violate them even once:

The first was to never accept anything as true which I could not accept as obviously true; that is to say, to carefully avoid impulsiveness and prejudice, and to include nothing in my conclusions but whatever was so clearly presented to my mind that I could have no reason to doubt it.

The second was to divide each of the problems I was examining in as many parts as I could, as many as should be necessary to solve them.

The third, to develop my thoughts in order, beginning with the simplest and easiest to understand matters, in order to reach by degrees, little by little, to the most complex knowledge, assuming an orderliness among them which did not at all naturally seem to follow one from the other.

And the last resolution was to make my enumerations so complete and my reviews so general that I could be assured that I had not omitted anything"

-René Descartes
(from the Discourse on the Method)

All we have discussed so far would turn out to be completely useless if at the end of it all we were to fail in the generation of the desired change in whatever form it was established: better financial results, being loved, loss of weight, etc.

As we head on towards the action stages of our improvement projects, we must be aware that the mere execution of the planned actions will not produce by itself the new habits and skills required to take our improvement efforts to new levels. Remember that behind our current patterns of behavior, there is one or more paradigms or beliefs giving us the assurance that whatever we are doing now is the right thing to do.

Therefore, in order to make our improvement efforts successful and permanent, we not only have to perform the necessary actions to generate the desired state in reality. We must also develop a change model that ensures that the paradigms holding in place the current way of doing things are identified and modified to produce the corresponding new behaviors.

Paradigms play a vital role in the way we understand and relate to the world. Altering or exchanging a paradigm that has been held for a long time is most definitely not something that can be done overnight. In fact, thinking that people will change instantly has been the most repetitive cause of failure we have detected in change projects.

Removing a paradigm is in many ways like removing a tooth: we will only take it out when we are totally convinced that there is no viable option to keep it and, once removed, unless we replace it with a new piece, all we will have to show for our efforts is a wonderful black hole in our mouth and a reduced ability to process our food.

Thus, once we enter into the execution phase of a change initiative, we must also actively engage in the creation of a change model capable of modifying or replacing the corresponding paradigms, as well as the adoption and development of its consequential principles, rules and patterns of behavior. This is what we really consider Change Management to be all about.

When we are learning a new language, we can only consider the new language truly assimilated when we have stopped "thinking" in our previous language and then translating the idea into the new one. Very similarly, a new paradigm is only really a part of us, only when we can operate continuously without having to recur to our previous governing paradigm.

Achieving this necessarily implies that in order to learn a new language we not only have to become actively involved in learning and practicing that language. We must also understand the way native speakers think before we can really make this new language an integral part of us. This must be the main goal of our change model.

8.1 Creating a Change Model

According to APICS (The American Production and Inventory Control Society), for individuals to be able to generate results using a new technology, they must go through the following stages (*19):

      1.- Contact

      2.- Awareness

      3.- Understanding

      4.- Positive Perception

      5.- Checking

      6.- Learning

      7.- Adoption

      8.- Adaptation

Since we adopted this very sequence for the creation of the change models that allow us the generation of results under new paradigms, we have come to understand that these eight stages must be visited at least twice during the life of a change initiative: first at a conceptual level and then again, during the execution of the implementation plans.

It is during the first visit that we become deeply involved with the situation by analyzing the problem, finding a solution, selling it to the key people and creating with them the necessary plans for its implementation.

The second visit happens when we execute our plans. As we begin to put our ideas into motion, we will come into contact with the actual place, people and conditions in which our solution will be implemented. This will undoubtedly trigger a more detailed awareness of the overall situation, which will in turn generate the need to re-study and re-think in greater detail the assumptions and proposals made while we were considering the problem at a conceptual level.

Then, a new "applied" understanding will arise followed by a new perception regarding the possibilities of our solution. As a result, the validity of the fundamental elements of the solution will have to be checked, and this will provide the whole team with the necessary opportunities to learn the subtleties of that particular situation in greater detail. This learning will then allow them to adopt a final solution and adapt it successfully to the specific reality at hand.

Even the simplest of change projects will suffice to demonstrate that neither the conceptual nor the practical processes advance in a linear way through the stages mentioned above. In fact, most of the times, we have found that many small looping cycles are needed at different stages before a change model can be successfully implemented.

Although many people consider these looping cycles inefficient, we have come to consider them one of the most important parts of the whole implementation process; because it is through them that the key people needed to ensure the progress of the project will clear their doubts, become comfortable with the solution, and help improve the proposed change model.

However, it must be said that it is also true that there is a great potential for big inefficiencies during this process of stepping back and forth while developing and implementing the solution, and it is precisely during these moments that the presence of the organization's leader is mandatory.

Despite all the hours spent during the analysis of the situation, and all the looping cycles to better understand and develop the solution during its execution, there will always be moments in which the decision to move forward will not be so clear, generating the never ending discussions of alternatives.

Many people, who participate very actively in the analysis and planning stages tend to disappear when the moment actually arrives to execute the plans that have been laid out. At first, we considered this attitude as a sign of lack of knowledge, commitment or interest on their part; but later on we discovered that people give execution the run around mainly because, due to the nature of change projects and the lack of real support from top management, it is during this stage that blame begins to be assigned in the most erratic of ways and fights between participants and the rest of the organization become inflamed.

Most of us know from bitter experiences that, participating in a change project is very much the equivalent of being the winner of a raffle in which the lucky winner gets to spend 5 minutes with a live tiger inside its cage. Surviving one of these projects without enemies or damage to our reputation has become a new form of art.

Only the presence and support of the organization's leader will provide the necessary trust throughout the whole organization to assume the risks and consequences of these initiatives without creating panic or finger pointing wars amongst every Function and Department.

Thus, if the new paradigm is to be taken seriously and the necessary new principles, rules and behaviors developed and adopted without having to recur to the old ways, the change model must have above anything else the full support and participation of the top management of the organization.

8.2 The most basic structure for a Change Model

During our fifteen years as change leaders, we have experimented with many different ways of structuring the teams in charge of implementing the change model. As a result of this experimentation, a common pattern began to emerge, leading us to the identification of four basic elements that must be present in order to ensure an efficient and successful change model implementation.

The decision makers and risk takers constitute the first element. Usually characterized, but not limited to top management, this element's function is to determine the goal of the project and then remove all obstacles (internal and external) that might block the progress of the team's efforts.

They must secure the necessary resources, sell the project internally, solve disputes as well as correct and smooth out damages caused by the implementation team. They are not expected to participate actively in the execution of the project's tasks because they play at a more strategic level.

The second element features the activity coordinators. These are the people in charge of continuously pushing forward the advancement of the project, making sure things happen one small step at a time, and removing any tactical obstacles that may get in the way. Although this function is usually delegated to the leader of the project, all top management must remain very involved and active in this role.

This group has as a main role the translation of all decisions and plans into simple and workable instructions for the rest of the organization. Other responsibilities include follow up and control, reporting, design and implementation of operating procedures and overall communication between the team members and with the rest of the organization.

The actual practical execution leaders comprise the third element. This is the group of people who will be in the battlefield leading the troops. These are usually the long seasoned generals who will be willing to do whatever is necessary to achieve their objective regardless of the cost or consequences.

They tend to be very charismatic leaders that inspire great respect from the troops, mainly because they obtain a very special pleasure from tackling difficult situations, which they see as personal challenges. They are completely action oriented and hate to get involved in philosophical discussions of any kind.

A very distinctive characteristic of this kind of person is that in times of peace, they find it very difficult not to get into fights with the rest of the organization. They need a reason to fight, and once they have embraced a cause you can be sure that they will take it to a safe end.

The fourth element consists of the actual "hands" of the project. These are the people that will actually get things done and constitute the larger mass of the project team.

This group will be mainly concerned with executing the tasks that are assigned to them in the best possible way while at the same time keeping their everyday jobs up to date. They will be the ones investing the extra hours needed to do both jobs, while attending training seminars and coordination meetings, providing all kinds of information for all kinds of reports, re-doing whatever the decisions makers miscalculated or adjusted, etc. In short, they are the real heroes behind every change project.

Depending on the size of the organization these four elements can be distributed in many different ways, but it is vital to make sure that every one of them is clearly understood and assigned before the execution stage begins.

8.3 The establishment of rules

In order to empower our teams to act efficiently and decisively towards the attainment of the specific improvements that are the objective of our change models, we must establish a basic set of rules before we get into the action stages of our project.

Bear in mind that as we begin to roll out our implementation plans, we will be altering the starting situation of the organization and a new reality will begin to emerge. As a consequence, change models take place mostly in unknown territories, and therefore, many decisions will have to be made in the field during the implementation stages in order to re-adapt the original plans to the new status of things.

Many leaders fail to see the need to set this specific set of rules for their projects, assuming that the overall working rules of the organization should be good enough to be used for everything that goes on in the company. However, because the most powerful change models need to challenge at least some of the existing paradigms of the organization, the generic, everyday working rules of the organization are usually not suited to facilitate the execution of change models. In fact, they tend to do exactly the opposite.

This is why, when establishing the basic rules for executing our change models, we must be aware that their main objective is to promote and facilitate the necessary decision making at the field level during the execution of the project and not to control everything that goes on in the project. If the implementation teams must recur to top management every time a decision regarding a modification to the original plans needs to be made, top management will very soon become the main constraining element for the progress of the project.

When we describe these guidelines as "a basic set of rules", we are trying to convey the message that we are talking about a handful of clear golden rules and not about an endless list of convoluted phrases that nobody in the organization can understand and apply to their specific reality.

It must be said that these basic rules will always be relative to the specific paradigms that are about to be changed, as well as to the particular situation in which the organization is submerged at the moment of implementing every specific change model. We have lived through enough experiences to know that the very same set of rules that works wonderfully for one project can seldom be transferred identically to another and produce the same results.

The fact that through the buy-in process we have already transferred ownership of the initiative to the key members of the organization, and that they have declared themselves willing to make it their own as a team is essential for the proper definition of the necessary rules.

Top management must provide all the guidance and counsel necessary to make sure the resulting operating rules are aligned with both the objective of the project and the culture of the organization, but any attempt from top management to take upon themselves the definition of these operating rules will most likely create more obstacles than provide valuable help.

The key members of the organization as a team, constantly checking for their validity with Top Management, then, must define the necessary operating rules. ALL RULES REGARDING A CHANGE MODEL MUST BE DOCUMENTED AND COMMUNICATED TO THE WHOLE TEAM AND TO TOP MANAGEMENT.

Although it sounds like such an obvious statement, it is surprising how many times we fail to do this simple act of synchronization. Some members of the team get together to solve an implementation obstacle, reach an agreement about a new operating rule to solve that specific problem and then totally forget to communicate their decision to the rest of the team or to top management.

A second mechanism to ensure that these rules, as well as other important implementation issues are correctly communicated to the whole team, is to have a quick meeting every day involving the heads of the project and the key personnel.

The reality is that setting up the rules for our change models constitutes a constant trial and error exercise during the life of the project. Some rules might apply for the entire duration of the project, while others might be valid only for a few hours. Some rules will apply to all members of the team, while others will only be applicable to certain few.

Remember, the objective of setting these golden rules is to ensure the proper empowerment of our team so that they can execute the implementation of the desired changes efficiently and decisively. These rules must be set and adjusted as needed, and keeping them updated is the responsibility of top management.

8.4 Developing a working discipline.

Once the project gets on its way, everyone in the organization, in and out of the implementation team, will be looking for signs regarding the kind of working discipline that will be used for this specific initiative. Mostly, they will look for these signs in the behavior, not in the words or emails, of the project leader and top management.

Because most of these projects represent an extra load of work for its team members, they will tend to corroborate the seriousness of this initiative by watching the project leader's behavior and then by matching their observations with top management's behavior.

If the leader attempts to implement a work discipline that differs significantly from the existing work culture of the organization, the typical first reaction from the team members will be to test her or his resolve by ignoring the new discipline and acting under the normal organizational culture.

This is a most natural reaction, and we should not interpret it as an act of sabotage by the team members. As change agents, we should handle this apparent resistance by providing very clear signs of our resolve and seriousness about this project and the ensuing adherence to the new working discipline.

The next normal reaction from the team members will be to check the instructions provided by the team leader with someone from top management. Usually, they will present them with a case in which they demonstrate that the new working discipline proposed by the project leader creates problems for the normal way of getting things done. More specifically, they will attempt to show that what the change agent is asking for will endanger the key results or measurements of one or more top managers.

In our experience, this is the moment of truth for the project. If, like it happens in most cases, Top Management falls into the temptation of going against the new working discipline, implemented by the team leader in order to avoid putting at risk their key measurements or results, it would be like infecting the project with cancer and only a miracle could give it some chance of success.

Just like children develop the ability to find the gaps in communication and principles between their parents to get their way, team members will constantly check for consistency between the instructions and working discipline of their project leader, their direct boss and the rest of top management.

We must bear in mind that given a conflict between complying with a task for their normal job and complying with a task for the change project, ninety nine percent of the time they will sacrifice compliance with the change project. The decision is rather simple: if they do not comply with the project task the worst that can happen, is that they will be severely reprehended; if they do not comply with a task for their normal job, they can be fired.

Therefore, developing an appropriate working discipline has little to do with becoming a tyrant that always chases his or her team members to obtain their maximum performance. It is about showing consistency and seriousness about our commitment to the project, as well as continuously gaining the support and help from all members of top management not only for the change model, but also for our own way to lead it.

8.5 Follow up and control.

When it comes to follow up and control, we have come to understand that this is a matter directly related to the very personal style of leadership of each individual. We have seen all sorts of methodologies and philosophies being used, sometimes successfully and some others unsuccessfully. Besides, the existing literature and educational programs in this field are so vast that we can hardly add anything new to what is already out there in all kinds of forms and languages.

However, there are three main issues that we feel the need to discuss in this book.

The first one has to do with drawing up a map or network of events that shows the chosen way to get from where we are to where we want to be. This network is important as a realistic base on which to support all implementation efforts and to demonstrate the logic and consistency of the proposed actions.

Like every other map, the main objective of this network of events is to help us to easily identify our position at any time during the execution of the project relative to where we are supposed to be, and with this information, take the necessary actions to re-take our chosen path.

Because the maps of change initiatives will mostly be drawn over uncharted territories, we have found of little use to draw very detailed maps at the beginning of the project. We will only have some reasonable degree of certainty about the initial conditions for the project, but as we attempt to draw further on the development of the project, our degree of uncertainty grows exponentially.

Maps of one hundred or more events become totally unmanageable. Changes in one single task may force us to re-draw the whole map. New information is difficult to reflect without creating a total havoc in the current schedule of our resources. And as leaders, we end up totally lost and making decisions based more on our gut feeling that on reliable information about the status of the project.

For this reason, we recommend that for change models, overall maps of the whole project should be drawn using only the main events or milestones of the initiative and not the minute detail of every single action.

As a very general rule of thumb, and having only our experience as justification, we look for initial maps of something between five and twenty events. As we move in time with our project, we can "zoom-in" on as much detail as needed in the upcoming events, for which we will have a better understanding and much clearer information.

The second aspect that we consider relevant regarding the follow up and control of change projects, is the way reports are usually provided about the degree of progress of each event or task.

It has become the standard practice to request and inform the degree of advancement of events or tasks in terms of a percentage relative to a given estimate. Because in order to provide a percentage, we must generate a second estimate (how much you reckon you have accomplished), we end up informing an estimate on an estimate, which is not precisely solid ground for managing our project.

If you allow us an oversimplification of the situation, we would like to refer you to a family example: when you take your children on a road trip, since they have no clear idea about the duration of the trip, they ask (a thousand times) two simple questions: are we there yet? how much longer will it take us to get there?

We would not think of answering something like: "we have advanced fifteen percent", right? What they are really asking is: When will they be able to start the next activity? Which they assume will be much more fun than just sitting still inside the car.

As project leaders, we are pretty much in the same situation: we want to know when will this task will be ready so that we can plan in greater detail the next events, and also get an updated estimate as to the final completion of the project.

Therefore, instead of asking for percentages of advancement, we should simply ask the two same questions as our children: are you done with this task? how much longer will it take you to finish it? This is the basic information we need to follow up and control our projects.

The third issue we should like to discuss involves the overall philosophy used for managing the evolution of the change model. Most people assume that as leaders of the project, our job is to ensure that each and every task is finished according to plan because this is the way to ensure that the overall project is finished on time.

Although this sounds straightforward enough, in reality it is not completely true. In most projects, there is at least one point in which two or more chains of events join each other (integration or assembly points). This means that only one of these chains of events will be part of the overall critical chain determining the total duration of the project.

As leaders of the project, we must focus our efforts on making sure that the events in this critical chain move forward at the best possible rate, because any delays in these tasks will cause the whole project to move further in time.

The methodology that describes this approach is called Critical Chain Project Management, and detailed information on it can be found in the book by Robert C. Newbold: "Project Management in the Fast Lane" (*20)

8.6 Do not be afraid to re-start if necessary.

It is essential to be fully aware that despite our best efforts to develop a solid change model and move it at a reasonable speed, we must always be on the alert to identify any signs telling us that we need to stop our implementation efforts and re-analyze the validity of our solution.

To begin with, there is always the possibility that the circumstances of the organization have been modified by external or internal factors, and as a consequence, the need to change has disappeared or has been modified substantially.

We recently experienced that case in a project where the internal changes were being provoked by the need to satisfy the negotiating style of the Purchasing Director of the main client of that organization. After years of holding his position, and without any warning that this could be possible, the Purchasing Director was transferred to another division rendering all the changes in process unnecessary.

It could also happen that as we enter into the execution stages, a clearer picture of the problem becomes available and further consequences of its elimination make it a dangerous thing to continue advancing with the project without re-analyzing this new information and developing the proper complements to the original solution to ensure that the strategic gains for the organization are not placed at risk.

The point is, that although it is not desirable to stop an ongoing effort to improve a certain aspect of our organization, we must always be conscious that the amount of resources available for improvement efforts in an organization are not infinite, and that even though we would like to improve many things at the same time, there will always be a limit on the number of issues we can attack effectively.

The most radical example we have experienced regarding this need to re-start an improvement initiative happened when after a year of strenuous efforts to implement an ERP solution (interlinked automation of the overall operations of an organization), it became clear that the chosen solution, as well as the consulting company hired to guide the implementation, were not suited to deal with the specific needs generated in this company by their unique business model.

Maybe you will wonder how it can be that it took an organization a whole year to realize the inappropriateness of their solution. Well, the fact is that these kinds of things happen very frequently when dealing with change projects, and we can tell you that we have seen companies deny this fact for much longer than only one year.

But the real lesson in this case is not why it took them that long to realize their mistake, but rather the fact that they did face the problem head on and were courageous enough to admit that their initial solution was not going to generate the desired results.

Sometimes the need to stop an improvement effort and re-align it with the company's goal is rather evident. Unfortunately, due to the fact that in all organizational endeavors there is always an element of politics and ego busting, the view of every initiative gets clouded with personal interests and points of view.

We have many times asked ourselves many times what the real difference is between being tenacious and being stubborn. Generally, we tend to assign the first adjective as a compliment to someone who is not easily discouraged from her or his target, while we usually apply the second one as a negative aspect of someone's personality. Of course, we would like to be thought of as "tenacious", while we would rather avoid being considered "stubborn". But what makes the difference between being called one thing or the other?

The best answer we have been able to produce so far is that the difference is not in what they do, but rather in what they accomplish. If you fail to generate the desired results, or better ones, you will be considered stubborn. On the other hand, if you end up triumphant showing the promised results in your hand, you will be judged as tenacious.

We believe this argument is relevant at this moment because "pulling the plug" on any improvement effort is a very delicate and difficult decision. Should we consider as sunken costs all the resources invested so far in a project that is not going the way we expected? Or should we invest some more resources in an attempt to bring it back to life?

Here again, the presence of the organizational leader becomes irreplace-able. Just like moving the project ahead requires the leader to assume its risks and consequences, the very same applies to deciding whether to stop the project and re-start if necessary. Only the organization's leader is suited to make this kind of decisions taking into account the balance between the overall benefits and consequences for the organization.

Chapter IX. Change, the only constant

"It is not the strongest of the species that survives, nor the most intelligent, but the one most responsive to change"
- Charles Darwin

"The dogmas of the quiet past are inadequate to the stormy present. The occasion is piled high with difficulty, and we must rise with the occasion. As our case is new, so we must think anew and act anew"
- Abraham Lincoln

Imagine for just a second that you were lucky enough to share life in paradise with Adam and Eve: You had eternal life and every beauty imaginable was yours to enjoy to your heart's content. Life was just perfect.

Then, on one afternoon, while you are taking a nap, Adam and Eve have a very interesting conversation with a snake, and as a result, they decide to have a go at the one thing that had been absolutely banned to you all, tasting the forbidden fruit.

When you wake up, you find out that every single aspect of your life has changed. You no longer live in paradise, your body feels different, all creatures are no longer friendly to you and worst of all, you are told that you will not live forever after all.

What would your reaction be to this sudden turn of events?, anger?, despair?, a sense of freedom?

Although this example is a very extreme, the fact is that every single minute the whole world is changing. Not as radically as from paradise to non-paradise, but it certainly happens at a speed that makes it very difficult for us to keep up with. And the more we expand our fields of knowledge, the more difficult it is to stay updated in all the matters that seem to be of interest to us.

The knowledge and skills that were essential for success just a short while ago have been either strongly questioned or rendered completely useless in the span of a few years like: pyramidal organizational structures, obtaining quality certifications, developing independent computing applications, buying securities from overseas sources, etc.

When it comes to personal, everyday matters, change has also forced us to keep learning new things all the time: sending messages through our cell phone, using digital cameras, programming microwave ovens, etc.

Whether we like it or not, change is happening all around us all the time. We might fight very strongly against it, and we might even manage to keep our personal world unchanged by developing an anti-change barrier around us. However, there is nothing we can do to stop the outside world from changing, which, sooner or later, will end up impacting our own secluded world.

As a consequence, if we fail to adapt our basic premises to the changes in our reality, the very same rules or behaviors that made us successful could very well be the same reason for our decline as leaders. Marshall Goldsmith, in his book "What got you here, won't get you there" (*21) makes the point very clearly:

> "If I can help you consider the possibility that, despite your demonstrable success and laudable self-esteem, you might not be as good as you think you are; that all of us have corners in our behavioral makeup that are messy; and that these messy corners can be pinpointed and tidied up, then I can leave the world -and your world- a slightly better place than we found it"

Change has been a matter of constant reflection and debate throughout history. Millions of pages have been written about it, from wonderful little stories like "Who moved my cheese" by Spencer Johnson, MD. (*22), to the more advanced scientific studies like the "Psychology of

Attitude Change and Social Influence" by Philip G. Zimbardo and Michael R. Leippe (*23).

At the moment of writing this book, typing the word "Change" in the books section of Amazon.com, produced 899,024 results. This means that we can never expect to know everything there is about change. But there is one thing we know for sure: change will continue to happen all around us and will continue to affect our lives in both, positive and negative ways. We do not know what the future will be like, but we are certain that it will be very different from what it is today.

Having lived our childhood and teens between the 60's and the 80's, we shared the wonder of our elders by experiencing the many "big firsts" of human kind during those years: the first human visit to the moon, the first color TV sets, the first video games, etc. Every single one of those events brought families and neighbors closer together, turning such experiences into "community happenings" that were enjoyed and talked about for many days afterwards.

Nowadays, we have new ways of making a big fuss about every "big experience" in the world: we now have e-Mail, Google, YouTube, Facebook, Messenger, Twitter, etc. that spread the word around the whole world in just a matter of minutes, turning every "big first" into a "world happening"

Change is not a matter of choice. Neither is it good or bad. Change simply happens, and it is up to us to decide what to make out of it.

9.1 The dilemma behind change

Adapting to change has been in the mind of human beings, consciously or unconsciously, during all our history. However, the real problem with change is that it poses a conflict every time we must decide about adapting -or not- to changes in matters that are really important to us.

When we become aware that something that matters to us has changed, our first impulse is to change in order to adapt ourselves to the new circumstances, and in this way, maintain or improve our status quo. For instance, if our competitors start to bring down their prices, we feel compelled to do the same in order to keep our share of the market intact. Or, if all our neighbors are getting new cars, we feel pressured to do the same.

In other words, in order to adapt to the changes around us, we feel the need to change ourselves. This sounds straightforward enough.

However, as we attempt to change ourselves, in order to adapt to the new circumstances, we realize that the same change that helps us to maintain our previous status quo intact, can or will have serious negative effects in other matters that are also important to us.

Following our competitors as they lower their prices might help us maintain our current share of the market, but it will also certainly have a negative impact in our margins and therefore in the profitability of our business.

Buying a new car to keep up appearances with our neighbors can also have a negative effect in our financial stability and then alter other important matters, like our long planned overseas vacations or even our retirement plans.

Thus, in order not to affect negatively other important matters, we feel the need not to change.

So the questions emerge: Should we change? Should we adapt to the changes around us? Or should we just acknowledge the changes, but remain the same? These questions get even more complicated by the amount and speed of changes going on around us all the time. How can we possibly keep up with every single change?

Then the most typical answer becomes obvious: Even though we are aware of the changes in our world, we choose not to adapt to every single changing situation until we really have to. We take on the challenge of adapting to one or two major changes in our lives, but other than that, we feel that all we can do about all the other changes is to hope that their possible impact in our lives will not be totally devastating.

That is how we all stack up a long list of pending issues to be resolved. We know they ought to be dealt with, but they just haven't reached the "must do" status.

From our research on this subject, we found the work by Efrat Goldratt (*24 and *25) to be one of the most accurate in the description of the dilemma generated by changing circumstances. She summarizes her findings in the following diagram:

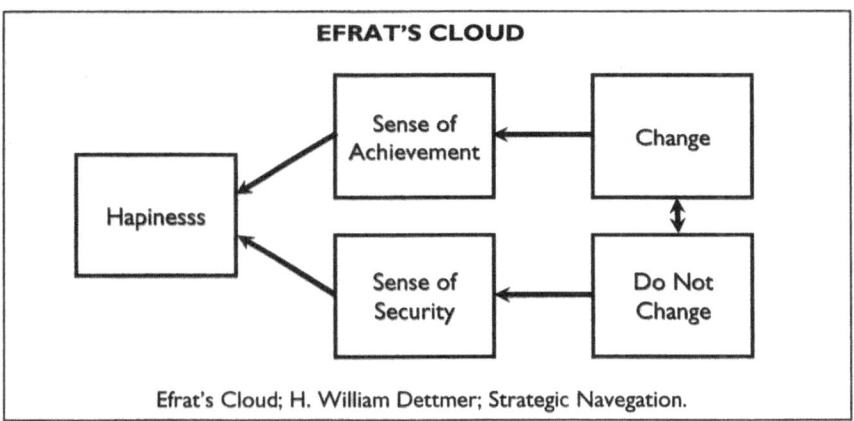

Fig 2.

In her view, we all share the goal of wanting to be happy. In order to be happy we must satisfy our need for achievement, and this demands us to embrace change. The bigger the change, the greater the sensation of achievement we get. On the other hand, to be happy, we must also satisfy our need for security. What is the point of achieving something if it is going to be taken away from you? Thus, in order to preserve security, we tend to resist change.

As discussed in Chapter IV, the way to break this kind of dilemma, is to dig deeper into our knowledge of the situation in order to find the beliefs and rules behind every logical connection. Why must we adapt to every change? Why must we endanger something else when we change?

Finding the answers to these questions will point us to the most basic beliefs driving our actions. By getting in the habit of working with our beliefs, instead of just aiming at our patterns of behavior and fighting many small battles simultaneously, we will find a more effective way to deal with many changes with only one adjustment.

9.2 Keep your basic assumptions in check

Our most basic beliefs play such a vital role as drivers of our instinctive behaviors that when we talk about adapting to changing circumstances, we are usually referring to changing some of our behaviors, and not necessarily about changing a root belief. It seems much easier to just change behaviors.

If our competitors are lowering their prices, we can just copy their behavior and, if that affects our profitability, all we have to do is to look for a change in another behavior that counters that impact in our margins, like buying cheaper raw material or using a more efficient distributor.

If our neighbors are buying new cars, we can also surely get a new model, and if that affects our financial stability, we will just have to cut down on some other expenses.

All of these are changes in behavior, and in some cases, these could very well be the proper way to go. However, if we want to go further in our analysis and find the root beliefs causing us to act in these ways, we should ask ourselves: why must we lower our prices in order to keep our share of the market? Why should we hurt our profitability by lowering our prices?

In this case, a possible belief pushing us to lower our prices could be that customers do not care about the quality of the product, and therefore, that their perception of value for this product is mainly determined by the price they have to pay. We all believed that this was precisely the case for all products that could be catalogued as commodities.

However, every now and then, someone challenges these very basic assumptions about a certain market or industry. This is the case for McDonald's, Starbucks, Zara, Best-Buy, etc. Instead of just copying the natural behaviors in their industries, they decided to challenge those very same assumptions rocking entire industries in the process.

You can be sure that taking on such a challenge was by no means easy or simple. And it is also true that these success stories represent only a small percentage of the total attempts to change root paradigms in any given market or industry. However, they do show the huge importance of always keeping in check our most basic assumptions about our business, our industry and life in general.

Working with the top management of a manufacturing company situated in the border between the USA and Mexico, we faced the typical symptoms of a badly administrated operation: many quality complaints from customers, loss of sales, high usage of overtime, low profitability, etc. After a deep analysis of the situation, we concluded that the root problem was the very high turnover rate of their personnel.

Further investigation showed that because of its location in the border between these two countries, the male workforce in this city switched jobs far too frequently, and this plant was 100% male manned. When we pointed the problem out to the owner of the company and presented the idea of adding women to their labor force, the response was: "This is very physically demanding work, women cannot possibly do it. Every attempt in the past to incorporate women into the workforce has ended up in accidents or machine breakdowns."

So, we went back to the plant and studied every process and yes, it certainly was very physically demanding work, but nothing that could not be handled by women provided the right mechanical aids and training were provided. This time, the response to the new proposal was: "Do you have any idea how much those mechanical aids cost? I am telling you that I am loosing money and you want me to spend more money in equipment!"

No, at the time we really had no idea of the cost of such equipment, but neither did he know how much money he was not earning due to the lack of that equipment, nor of the hidden costs this generated. Together, we did the necessary math exercises and, in the end, we found out that the necessary investment in mechanical aids to substitute the unstable male labor force would pay itself off in less than six months, bringing in after that period a very interesting sum of extra profits.

The solution had been there all the time, right in front of their very eyes, but a rooted paradigm like: "this is a man's job", stopped them from updating their knowledge about the possible acquisition of mechanical aids to make the work manageable for women.

9.3 By now you might be wrong

We must always be aware of the governing beliefs behind our behaviors in the matters that we consider most important: the education of our children, marriage, business, leadership, etc., and we must also be willing to review and update them as the need arises, based on the results we are obtaining now and on the results we want for our future.

It really does not matter much how effective our paradigms were in the past. We must always look at them in the light of the current and the foreseeable circumstances, and then value them according to their effectiveness under those circumstances.

A friend who has made his living buying and selling shares on the stock exchange, told us once that he reviews his portfolio every day and asks himself the following question about every share he owns: if I did not already have this share, would I buy it today? If the answer is no, he knows it's time to sell it.

Knowing what you know about life today, would you have studied the same career?, would you have studied a career at all?, would you have started a business sooner?, would you have treated your parents differently?

After fifteen years of working with a great variety of organizations, we are still surprised at how many things are considered erroneous by the current management, and yet they still fight to perpetuate the very same system and pass it on to the next generation: performance measurement systems, creation of silos in each department, lack of commitment to agreements amongst managers, etc.

Curiously enough, we tend to do exactly the same when it comes to the education of our children. Even though we did not like many of the things our parents did to us, we end up doing exactly the same things to our children.

Be aware that by the time we decide and execute any given idea, both our solution and the circumstances around it will most likely have evolved, because our mind and the changes in the surrounding environment tend to evolve at faster speeds than our ability to execute our plans.

This generates a series of practical complications that are very difficult to manage, since once again we are faced with a dilemma regarding our possible reaction: should we be firm in the execution of the original solution? or, should we adapt our solution to every change we find along the way?

At the heart of all our improvement efforts there must be an awareness that reality as we perceive it, given our mental patterns and models, is only a personal interpretation of the circumstances we can detect and that are in constant evolution.

If we truly want to leave a better world than the one we found, we must make sure that the next generation's behavior is guided by better suited beliefs than the ones we inherited. We must have the courage to challenge and break free from the patterns that have clouded our lives and develop new paradigms that can take the next generations a step further in their search for happiness.

We strongly believe that one such change of paradigm starts by questioning the validity of the belief that "being right is enough" and working hard on developing a new paradigm: "BEING RIGHT, IS NOT ENOUGH!"

Welcome to our journey.

Bibliography.

Chapter I:

*1 Benjamin Franklin; The Art of Virtue; Acorn Publishing; Eden Praire, Minnesota; Second Edition 1990; pp41

Chapter II:

*2 Stephen Covey; The Seven Habits of the Highly Successful People, Powerful lessons in personal change; Free Press; New York; 1989, 2004

*3 Robert C. Newbold; The Billion Dollars Solution, Secrets of Prochain project management; Prochain Press; 2008

Chapter III:

*4 Robert F. Bennett; Gaining Control, Your key to Freedom and Success; Franklin Quest Co.; Salt Lake City, Utah; 1987; pp 61

*5 Keith R. McFarland; The Breakthrough Company, How everyday companies become extraordinary performers; Crown Business; New York; 2008; pp28

*6 H. William Dettmer; Strategic Navigation, A systems approach to business strategy; Quality Press; American Society for Quality; Milwaukee; 2003

Chapter IV:

*7 The Power of Vision; Joel Barker (Video) CHIV

*8 Roger Martin; The Opposable Mind, How successful leaders win through integrative thinking; Harvard Business School Press; Boston; Massachusetts; 2007

*9 Robert B. Dilts, Todd Epstein, Robert W. Dilts; Tools for Dreamers, Strategies for creativity and the structure of innovation; Meta Publications; 1991

*10 Eli Schragenheim; Management Dilemmas, The Theory of Constraints approach to problem identification and solutions; St. Lucie Press; APICS Series on Constraints Management; 1999

Chapter V:

*11 Mahan Khalsa; Let's Get Real or Let's Not Play, The demise of dysfunctional selling and the advent of helping clients succeed; White Water press; 1999; pp14

*12 Neil Rackham; SPIN Selling; McGraw-Hill; 1988; pp53-98

*13 Keith M. Eades; Solution Selling, The revolutionary sales process that is changing the way people sell; McGraw-Hill; 2004; pp85-130

Chapter VI:

*14 William H. Dettmer; Breaking the Constraints to World Class Performance; Quality Press; American Society for Quality; Milwaukee; 1998

*15 Lisa J. Scheinkopf; Thinking for a Change, Putting the TOC thinking processes to use; St. Lucie Press; APICS Series on Constraints Management; 1999

*16 Tony Buzan, Barry Buzan; The Mind Map Book, How to use radiant thinking to maximize your brain's untapped potential; Plume; 1996

Chapter VII:

*17 Keith R. McFarland; The Breakthrough Company, How everyday companies become extraordinary performers; Crown Business; New York; 2008; pp27-28

*18 Eliyahu M. Goldratt and Jeff Cox; The Goal, A process of ongoing improvement; Second revised edition; North River Press; Great Barrington; Massachustes; 2004

Chapter VIII:

*19 Introduction to ERP; APICS

*20 Robert C. Newbold; Project Management in the Fast Lane, Applying the Theory of Constraints; St. Lucie Press; APICS Series on Constraints Management; 1998; pp55-114

Chapter IX:

*21 Marshall Goldsmith; What got you here, won't get you there, How successful people become even more successful; Hyperion; New York; 2007

*22 Spencer Johnson, MD; Who Moved my Cheese?, An a-mazing way to deal with change in your work and in our life; G.P. Putman's Sons; New York; 1998

*23 Philip G. Zimbardo and Michael R. Leippe; Psychology of Attitude Change and Social Influence; McGraw-Hill; 1991

*24 Efrat's Cloud; Efrat Goldratt

*25 H. William Dettmer; Strategic Navigation, A systems approach to business strategy; Quality Press; American Society for Quality; Milwaukee; 2003; pp117